The Preschooler's BUSY BOOK

Meadowbrook Press

Distributed by Simon & Schuster
New York

Library of Congress Cataloging-in-Publication Data
Kuffner, Trish.
    The preschooler's busy book: 365 creative games and activities to
occupy your 3-to-6-year-old / by Trish Kuffner.
    p. cm.
    Includes bibliographical references (p.) and index.
    ISBN 0-88166-351-4. — ISBN 0-671-31633-8 (S&S)
    1. Creative activities and seat work. 2. Education, Preschool. I. Title.
LB1140.35.C74K844   1998
372.5—dc21   98-29639
                                                   CIP

Editor: Liya Lev Oertel
Production Manager: Joe Gagne
Desktop Publishing: Danielle White
Cover Art: Dorothy Stott
Illustrations: Laurel Aiello

© 1998 by Patricia Kuffner

Published by Meadowbrook Press, 5451 Smetana Drive; Minnetonka,
Minnesota 55343

BOOK TRADE DISTRIBUTION by Simon & Schuster, a division of Simon
and Schuster, Inc., 1230 Avenue of the Americas, New York, NY 10020

08   19 18

Printed in the United States of America

Dedication

For my husband, Wayne,
and our four precious children,
Andria, Emily, Joshua, and Johanna.

I have learned far more from you
than you will ever learn from me.

Table of Contents

Introduction

If I Had My Child to Raise Over Again

If I had my child to raise over again,
I'd fingerpaint more and point the finger less.
I'd do less correcting and more connecting.
I'd take my eyes off my watch, and watch with my eyes.
I would care to know less and know to care more.
I'd take more hikes and fly more kites.
I'd stop playing serious, and seriously play.
I'd run through more fields and gaze at more stars.
I'd do more hugging and less tugging.
I would be firm less often, and affirm much more.
I'd build self-esteem first, and the house later.
I'd teach less about the love of power, and more
       about the power of love.
—*Diane Loomans*

Although coping with the needs of a baby can be tough for new parents, it usually doesn't take long for most to feel comfortable with changing, feeding, holding, and rocking their infants. As babies grow into toddlers, most parents are able to cope with wiping noses and behinds, making meals no one eats, finding toys and clothes and sticky finger marks everywhere, and, of course, doing laundry, laundry, laundry. But as children leave the toddler stage and become full-fledged preschoolers, their needs change dramatically. Few parents feel prepared to meet the daily demands of life with a preschooler, and most find it a constant challenge to meet their physical, mental, emotional, and spiritual needs.

I first encountered life with a preschooler during an exceptionally rainy, coastal Canadian winter. Andria, my oldest daughter, was three. Her sister. Emily, was almost two, and baby Joshua was not yet six months old. Emily was in the midst of toilet training, and Josh nursed at least every two hours. Andria, normally sweet-tempered and easy-to-please, was becoming difficult. As the rain continued, her moodiness increased. She needed new things to do, new experiences to stimulate her, but most of my time and energy went into meeting the needs of the two younger children. As the days dragged on, and our frustration festered, I entertained a multitude of doubts about my ability (or lack thereof) to be a good mother. I had always heard about "quality time" with your child; I seemed to have an awful lot of quantity time without much quality!

While I knew I couldn't always expect to drop everything to get involved with her, I knew there must be something I could do to provide my preschooler with a more creative and stimulating environment. I knew there must be activities that would both challenge and entertain her. I wanted ideas for little projects we could work on together, but I also wanted things she could do on her own while I was busy elsewhere. Since we were living on one income, I also needed activities that made use of basic items we already had around the house.

I started to reorganize our home to better meet the changing needs of our family. I began collecting and saving all kinds of interesting things that we could use in our activities. I became much more organized and tried to plan for special things we could do together. I also relaxed a little and learned to enjoy my children and their small and simple pleasures. Confidence in my parenting abilities returned as I began to feel in control again.

While I don't claim to be a "specialist" of any sort, my experiences at home, all day, every day, with three very young children, taught me much about what works and what doesn't. This book is a compilation of the ideas and activities that met my needs as a parent, as well as the needs of my children, during those challenging preschool years. It contains suggestions for every situation and occasion, for both indoors and out, for summer and winter, for quiet times and not-so-quiet times. Although this book is written by a stay-at-home mom as a resource for others in the same situation, be assured that it is well-suited for anyone who has a preschooler in their life: mothers or fathers, grandparents, aunts or uncles, babysitters, daycare workers, preschool teachers, church workers, or playgroup leaders. If you are looking for one good book on what to do with a preschooler and how to do it, this book is indeed for you.

While many ideas in this book may continue to entertain your children long after the preschool stage, the activities in this book are most suitable for children between the ages of three and six. Because abilities of children in that age range vary greatly, some ideas will be too advanced for a three-year-old, and some will be too simple for a five- or six-year-old. Use your judgment in choosing activities that best meet the capabilities and interests of your child, and be prepared to supervise when necessary.

A note on the use of "his" and "her"; in recognition of the fact that children do indeed come in both genders, and in an effort to represent each, the use of the male and female pronouns will alternate with each chapter.

"It will be gone before you know it. The fingerprints on the wall appear higher and higher. Then suddenly they disappear."
—*Dorothy Evslin*

Enjoy your preschooler! Although it may seem at times that they will never grow up, they always do. The long, seemingly endless days will gradually be replaced by days with not enough hours in them. Children who once needed you for everything will need you less and less, and the days of leisurely walks, playdough and afternoon naps will be a warm and fuzzy memory. My hope is that both you and your child will have many happy hours of playing, growing, and learning together.

Trish Kuffner

CHAPTER 1

Help! I Have a Preschooler!

"To be a good housewife and mother, you have to be more self-generated. You have to create your own playground of the imagination, and the mind. To be a really good, creative mother you have to be an extraordinary woman. You have to keep yourself involved with your child during great periods of the day when it's just the two of you and you feel that at any moment you may literally go out of your mind."
—*Meryl Streep*

Preschoolers! They don't emerge overnight, or on their third birthday. It may happen so slowly, you hardly notice it at all, but one day you realize that your clumsy, confusing little toddler is gone. In his place is an energetic, intensely curious, sometimes determined (some might call it stubborn), very adventurous little child. Chances are he is out of diapers, off the bottle, and somewhat able to take a little responsibility for himself. He probably knows the rules of the house, and doesn't need constant monitoring. After a few years of babies and toddlers, parents often find the preschool stage quite refreshing.

But while life with a preschooler can be a celebration, you will always have days when it seems more like a chore. We all have bad days, and children are no exception. Your child may be a wonderful little person most of the time, but his boundless energy and relatively short attention span may result in some irritating, demanding, and temperamental behavior. While providing your child with lots of fun and interesting things to do won't solve all his behavior problems, it may help prevent some of the signs and symptoms of boredom that result from a lack of appropriate stimulation.

There are many ways to stimulate your child. At around age three, children often enter a preschool or playgroup for two or more days a week. A group such as this will usually provide your child with new friends and a new outlet for his creativity and energy. If your child spends all his time at home with you or another caregiver, he relies on you for new experiences, outings, and creative activities. His day needs some structure—a loose schedule with recognizable breaks. He needs to meet people of different ages—adults and children alike. He relies on you to introduce him to books and music, arts and crafts projects, rambunctious games, and quiet learning activities. A short walk or some outdoor play should be part of every day.

While a variety of experiences and activities are essential to your child's development, resist the urge to push him too hard. All children need lots of time for creative and spontaneous play. Rather than assuming the role of teacher, instructing and directing your child, try to act as his helper in the learning process. Children need to learn on their own and to run their own show, while knowing that you are there to help them when and if they need it. Children who have learned to direct their own play, who have been given lots of time to be creative and to use their imaginations, are less likely to experience boredom than those whose time has been rigidly planned for them.

"BUT THERE'S NOTHING TO DO!"

All children, no matter how creative, imaginative and self-sufficient, will at one time or another experience a case of boredom or restlessness. Here are some suggestions to help you alleviate boredom in your preschooler.

Keep a Baker's Box in the kitchen.

Whether you're in the kitchen a little or a lot, your child will naturally want to be with you when you are. Kitchen cupboards and drawers are full of interesting things that may prove irresistible to your child. Why not provide your child with his very own Baker's Box? Put together a collection of unbreakable kitchen tools in a plastic crate or small storage box. Store it in a spare cupboard that is low enough for your child to reach on his own. He can use his tools for play or for doing some "real" cooking or baking with you. Some suggestions for a Baker's Box are

cake pan • cake rack • cookie cutters • cookie sheet •
large metal or plastic bowl • measuring spoons • muffin
tin • pie plate • plastic measuring cups • rubber spatula
• wooden spoon

Have a Busy Box handy.

A spare kitchen cupboard low enough for your child to reach
is an ideal spot for his very own Busy Box. Fill a small storage
box or plastic crate with things that he can do on his own, any
time he wants. Good things to keep in a Busy Box are

child-safe scissors • coloring books • construction paper
• cookie cutters • crayons • glue • ink pad with ink
stamps • paper • playdough • stickers • tape

Make a Job Jar for your child.

Whether you are a working Mom, an at-home Dad, a loving
grandparent, or an occasional babysitter, sometimes you will
have household chores to do while your preschooler is
around. Providing a job jar for your child gives him something
to do while you work, and can also help instill in him a sense
of responsibility toward household chores.

You can make a job jar for your child out of an empty jar,
coffee can, or small box. Cut strips of paper and on each one
print a small job that needs to be done; for example,
straighten the bookshelves, wash the bathroom sink, put away
the towels, wash the vegetables, pick up the toys, and so on.

You will know the jobs your child is capable of doing with minimum supervision and assistance. If your child is normally an unwilling helper, allowing him to chose his own job may also help reduce some of his reluctance.

Take along a Busy Bag.

Be prepared for those times when you just have to wait—at the doctor's office, at the hairdresser's, or in a restaurant. Turn a drawstring bag or backpack into a take-along Busy Bag that can be filled with special things to keep your child amused. Some suggestions for a Busy Bag are

coloring books and paper • crayons and markers • dolls and associated clothing, blankets, bottles, and other accessories • ingredients for an Edible Necklace (see page 109); shoestring licorice and cereal or crackers with holes in the middle • magnets and a small metal cake pan (see Magnet Fun, page 108) • matchbox cars • puzzles • special snacks • stickers and a sticker book

Use your imagination when filling the Busy Bag. Do it yourself, so the contents will be a surprise for your child, or have your child help you fill the bag before you go.

Rotate your child's toys.
In their first few years of life, most children receive many wonderful toys as gifts for birthdays, Christmas, or other occasions. I have always appreciated the good intentions of the givers, but at the same time have been saddened to see such wonderful toys used and played with so rarely. Expensive store-bought toys certainly are nice, but your child will lose interest in even the most creative toys when they are always around. By rotating toys every four to six weeks, they will seem new to him and will be interesting and exciting all over again.

To begin toy rotation, separate your child's toys into piles (if your child has a favorite toy, keep it out all the time). Keep one pile in your child's play area, and pack the others away in boxes, marking on them the dates they are to be brought out. This system will also work well for your child's books.

Make a Crazy Can.
You've probably all been there—5 P.M., dinner nowhere near prepared, a nursing baby in one arm, a cranky toddler hanging onto one leg, and a whiny, demanding preschooler looking for something to do. Now is not the time for fingerpaints or papier-mâché! Now is not the time to brainstorm ideas for exciting and creative things to do with a four-year-old. What you can do is be prepared ahead of time with a Crazy Can.

Make a list of on-the-spot activities that require no special materials, need no time-consuming preparation or cleanup, and above all, demand no large amount of adult participation or supervision. Write down these ideas on index cards or small pieces of paper and place them inside an empty coffee can. (If you like, decorate the can with cheerful contact paper, or cover it with plain paper and have your child decorate it with paints, markers, or crayons.) When things start to get crazy (or when there's just "nothing to do"), choose a card from the can for an instant remedy. Appendix B, page 366, offers a suggested list of activities appropriate for your Crazy Can.

Look for new activities and experiences.
While children need free time for creative play, they also rely on you to introduce them to new projects, activities, and adventures. This is hard to do on the spur of the moment, so some advance planning on your part is required. Try to schedule one or two fun, challenging, and creative activities each day. Decide on the activities ahead of time, and have all the necessary supplies assembled in advance. Read on for some additional advice on planning activities for your child.

PLANNING YOUR ACTIVITIES

Failing to plan is planning to fail, and that can apply to the big stuff, like saving for your child's education, as well as the little stuff, like starting a new art project or playing a game with your child. Recognize the importance of planning new and creative activities. You can have a shelf full of books on activities for children, or just this one, but the ideas this book contains are only valuable to you and your child if you use them (and if you don't do a little advance planning, chances are that you won't use them). Here are some helpful steps for planning your activities.

1. Read this book from cover to cover, and fill a weekly planner with activities you would like to try for each day. You can use a copy of the Weekly Activity Planner on page 14 or use your own calendar. Include a few alternate activities for when the weather won't cooperate or when things are just not right for what you have planned.
2. Use your weekly activity plan to make a list of supplies you will need, and assemble or purchase them beforehand.
3. Make a list of what you need to prepare before your child becomes involved in the activity—mix paint, draw a treasure hunt map, and so on.
4. Plan special activities when your child is with a babysitter, and have all the necessary materials handy. This will let your sitter know that a day or night of TV watching is not an option.
5. Make a list of ideas that would be fun to do anytime you can fit them into your schedule. Have this list ready when you have some unexpected free time.

STOCKING YOUR CRAFT CUPBOARD

Whether you have a cupboard to spare, or just a box in the basement somewhere, here are some items you should have on hand for the various activities described in this book.

Things to save:

aluminum foil • aluminum pie plates (various sizes) • bottle caps • boxes • brown paper bags • buttons • candles • cardboard • catalogs • cereal boxes • chopsticks • clothespins • coffee cans with lids • coins • confetti • corks • cotton balls • cotton batting • cotton swabs • dried beans • dried pasta (different shapes and sizes) • egg cartons • egg shells • empty jars and lids • envelopes • fabric scraps • felt • greeting cards (used) • junk mail • lids from plastic gallon jugs • magazines • metal lids from frozen juice cans • newspapers • old clothes and costume jewelry for dress-up • old mittens, socks, and gloves for puppets • old telephone books • old toothbrushes • paint sample chips • paper clips • paper muffin cup liners • paper plates/cups/bowls • paper scraps • paper towel/toilet paper tubes • photographs of friends and family • pine cones • plastic bowls, lids, bottles • playing cards • popcorn • Popsicle sticks • ribbon • rice (uncooked) • rubber bands • ruler • sandpaper • shoelaces • sponges • spray bottle • stickers

of all kinds • string • Styrofoam trays • swizzle sticks •
thread • thread spools • toothpicks • wood scraps •
wrapping paper scraps • yarn scraps

Things to buy:

art smock (or use an old shirt) • beads • chalk • child-
safe scissors • construction paper in various colors • craft
magnets • crayons • crepe paper • glitter • glue or glue
sticks • googly eyes • hole puncher • masking tape •
newsprint pads or rolls • paper clips • paper fasteners •
pencil crayons • pencil sharpener • pencils • pens • pipe
cleaners • plain writing pads • ruler • self-adhesive paper
• stapler • stickers • straws • tempera paints and brushes
• tissue paper • transparent tape • washable markers

WHAT ABOUT TELEVISION?

For me, the key to the whole "children and television" issue is not so much what the children watch, because we can control that. My main concern about children and television is more about how parents use television in their home, and what children do not do when they watch television. It is easy to use the television as a babysitter on occasion, but it can be habit-forming to both parent and child. The few short years of early childhood can quickly be gobbled up by thousands of hours of TV viewing—time that could and should have been spent playing, reading, walking, talking, painting, crafting: time spent together.

But television, for better or worse, is here to stay. As parents we can control it and use it in such a way that it will be beneficial to our child's development and to the parent/child relationship. First of all, be selective in what your children watch. Good television programs can make learning fun and can expand your child's knowledge of the world. Programs like *Sesame Street* can even help your child get ready for school. On the other hand, many programs on television today are far from innocent or educational and can be very detrimental to our children's emotional, intellectual, and spiritual well-being. So choose wisely; look for programs or videotapes that instruct, entertain, and reinforce the values and principles you wish to develop in your child.

Second, limit your child's viewing time each day. Remember, time spent watching TV is time that your child does not spend on other, more valuable, activities, such as playing games, reading (or being read to), or using his imagination in countless other ways. Children who spend a lot of time watching television can come to expect the instant stimulation that a fast-paced show can bring, and may be less likely to use their own imagination and creativity to stimulate themselves.

Third, when possible, watch television with your child. Most programs move at such a fast pace that children have a hard time keeping track of the content. It is almost impossible for children to stop and ponder what is being presented. Parents can provide connections that the children miss. By reminding your child of related events in his own life, you help him make sense of what he sees.

Finally, set an example for your child. Show him that you would rather read a book or play a game or talk to him than watch TV. It's hard to expect your child to learn to limit his viewing and choose programs wisely when you do just the opposite. Remember, children learn from our actions more than our words.

A WORD OF ENCOURAGEMENT

"Motherhood brings as much joy as ever, but it still brings boredom, exhaustion, and sorrow too. Nothing else will ever make you as happy or as sad, as proud or as tired, for nothing is quite as hard as helping a person develop his own individuality—especially while you struggle to keep your own."
—*Marguerite Kelly and Elia Parsons*

Be encouraged as you weather the stormy seas of parenting. Raising a child is a monumental task that brings with it a great amount of work, but you need not (and should not!) spend 100 percent of your time catering to the needs or wants of your preschooler. By providing your child with daily activities that are simple and fun, by placing more importance on your child's happiness and learning than on the appearance of your home, and by talking to your child on a level he understands, you help him become more capable and confident. Not only will he be better prepared for school when the time comes, but, in the process, you help to make many happy memories of childhood.

Weekly Activity Planner

Week of:

To Do	To Buy
Monday _____ _____ _____	_____ _____ _____ _____
Tuesday _____ _____ _____	_____ _____ _____ _____
Wednesday _____ _____ _____	_____ _____ _____ _____
Thursday _____ _____ _____	_____ _____ _____ _____

Weekly Activity Planner

Week of:

To Do	To Buy
Friday _____ _____ _____	_____ _____ _____ _____
Saturday _____ _____ _____	_____ _____ _____ _____
Sunday _____ _____ _____	_____ _____ _____ _____
Rainy Day Options _____ _____ _____	_____ _____ _____ _____

CHAPTER 2
Rainy Day Play

"The years rush past, as every older woman will tell the young mothers who complain that they still have two little ones at home and it seems like forever before they will all be in school. Oh no, they say, time flies—enjoy them while they're young— they grow up so fast. . . .

The mothers agree that indeed the years do fly. It's the days that don't. The hours, minutes of a single day sometimes just stop. And a mother finds herself standing in the middle of a room wondering. Wondering. Years fly. Of course they do. But a mother can gag on a day."
—*Jain Sherrard*

Life with preschoolers can be a wonderful, rewarding experience. On long, warm, summer days, when adults and children alike can be outside from sunup to sundown, parenting can seem very fun and easy. But "fun" and "easy" are not words you are likely to hear from anyone who has endured a week of rain with several house-bound preschoolers. Most preschoolers have a great amount of energy, but a relatively short attention span. Boredom can cause acutely irritating behavior in small children and should be avoided as much as possible. Now is the time for big, messy art projects (see Chapter 8) and marathon baking sessions.

Invite friends for lunch frequently, and always be prepared with something fun for the children to do indoors. Some of the activities that follow require a table or countertop, and some require water—these are best-suited to your kitchen. Other water-related activities are a natural for the bathroom and bathtime. The rest are more flexible, and can be easily adapted to the bedroom, living room, family room, or other room in the house that has plenty of floor space and an absence of breakables.

Clean Coins

Old toothbrush
Soap
Water
Bowl
Coins
Dishcloth or paper towel
Salt and vinegar (optional)

Your child can practice cleaning coins with an old toothbrush and some soap and water. Fill a bowl with a small amount of water and place a few coins in the bowl. Your child will have fun brushing the coins with soap to make them look brand new. When the coins are as clean as your child can make them, dry them with a dishcloth or paper towel.

For super-shiny coins, mix a small amount of salt and vinegar in a bowl. Drop the coins in and watch the tarnish fade. (If you do use vinegar, make sure your child does not get any in her eyes; soap is bad enough, but vinegar will really sting!)

Super Suds

Liquid detergent
Water
Bowl
Eggbeater
Straw (optional)

Put a few drops of liquid detergent into a bowl and fill it half-way with water. Use an eggbeater to whip up some suds in the soapy water, or a big straw to blow some really big bubbles. This also works well at the kitchen sink; fill the sink with soapy water and pull up a chair for your child to stand on as she plays.

As a variation, fill a sink with warm soapy water; give your child spoons, a whisk, and plastic bowls and dishes, and let her have fun with water.

Musical Glasses

Drinking glasses
Water
Spoon

Fill drinking glasses with different amounts of water and have your child lightly tap the glasses with a spoon. Notice the different sounds each glass makes. Try to play simple tunes, or make up your own melodies as you play.

Washing Windows

Spray bottle
Water
Vinegar
Cleaning cloth

Fill a spray bottle with water and ¼ cup white vinegar. Give your child the bottle and cleaning cloth and let her help you wash the windows, bathroom counters, or kitchen appliances. She will love to be your helper and work along side you while you do some of your own cleaning.

Soap Pal

Bar of soap
Washcloth
Thread
Needle
Fabric or felt scraps

Make bathtime more fun by providing your child with her very own soap pal. Wrap a washcloth around a bar of soap and sew the open ends together, encasing the soap completely. Cut eye shapes out of fabric or felt, and sew the eyes on top of the soap bundle. If you like, sew on a mouth, nose, eyebrows, and any other details for more fun. Then give your child the soap pal and let her lather up in the bath.

Bath Paints

This game is an all-time favorite with our children, but merits a few words of caution. If you have ceramic tile in your bathtub area, you may want to skip this one, as the food coloring may stain the grout. If your child has sensitive skin, the shaving cream (depending on the brand) can cause irritation. In any case, children will almost certainly need another bath after this activity!

Shaving cream
Food coloring
Muffin tin
Spoon
Paintbrushes or sponge

Squirt shaving cream into the individual sections of a muffin tin. Add a few drops of food coloring to each section and mix with a spoon. The kids will love painting the walls, the tub, and themselves with their hands, a sponge, or paintbrushes. Older children will enjoy mixing the colors to create new ones. Clean up is easy when the fun ends—just hose down the tub, with your child in it!

Water Rainbow

Eyedropper
Small containers of water
Food coloring in rainbow colors

Give your child an eyedropper and several small containers of water colored with a few drops of food coloring. Let her arrange the colors to create a rainbow, mix colors, or drop water into other empty containers.

Count the Coins

Pennies or other coins

Give your child a jar of pennies or other coins and have her count them and place them in stacks of five or ten. Then count the stacks. Talk to her about what money can and cannot buy by giving her examples: "Can money buy us food?" "...good friends?" "...clothes?" "...a new baby sister?"

Indoor Sandbox

Cardboard box or plastic baby bath
Puffed wheat or rice cereal
Sandbox toys

Create an indoor sandbox by filling a cardboard box or plastic baby bath or basin with inexpensive puffed wheat or rice cereal. Use buckets, shovels, and dump trucks, or measuring cups, spoons, and bowls. (Uncooked rice can be inexpensive when bought in bulk, and it makes an interesting road surface for small trucks or other wheeled toys.)

Paper Punch

Hole punch
Paper scraps

Give your child a hole punch and scraps of paper in various colors. She will amuse herself for quite some time making confetti that can be saved and used for arts and crafts activities.

Sharpen a Pencil

Although you may not think that this activity would hold your child's attention for long, you may be surprised!

Pencils or crayons
Pencil or crayon sharpener
Small plate or cup

Your preschooler will no doubt have a lot of fun sharpening pencils. Give her a pencil sharpener, a pencil, and a small plate or cup to catch the shavings. For younger children, use crayons and a crayon sharpener. (Save the crayon shavings for making Stained-Glass Crayons, page 173, Rainbow Crayons, page 174, or Wax Paper Art, page 244.)

Nail Board

Nails
Wooden board
Hammer
String or elastic bands

Hammer nails into a piece of board. Allow your child to create
a design by wrapping string or colored elastic bands around
the nails. Hammer the nails in a pattern, or use rows or
circles so your child can create her own designs. Make sure
that the nails only penetrate the top side of the board, put
away the hammer and excess nails, and supervise your child to
avoid accidents.

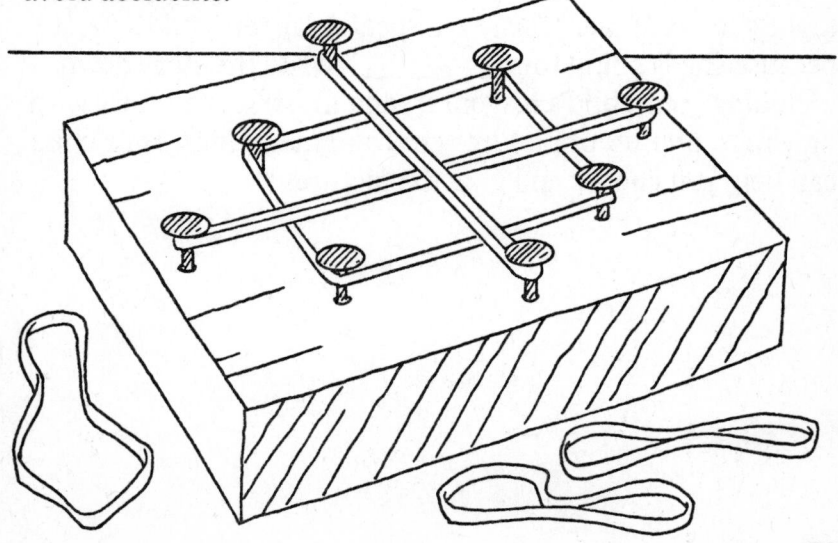

Write a Story

Look in your local library for information on making books with children. Stories turned into books will be treasured for years to come.

Paper
Pen, markers, or crayons
Photographs or old magazines
Scissors
Glue

Write a story with your child about events in her life—a story in which she is the central character. Begin the story by saying, for example, "Today is a special day for (child's name) because she is going to _____." Write the story down, including your child's responses, and illustrate the story with drawings, photos, or pictures cut from magazines. Your child can help you choose and glue the pictures.

Indoor Tent

Sheet or blanket
Empty table

Place a sheet or blanket over a table to make an indoor tent. Put a special snack inside and give your child a flashlight. If you like, furnish the tent with pillows and a blanket, and let your child camp out all morning.

What's Missing?

Various household objects or small toys

Test your preschooler's memory skills by placing a few toys or household objects in front her. Allow her to study them, then have her close her eyes while you remove one object. See if she can tell you which object is missing.

Sticker Play

Stickers from magazine and record clubs

Save all stickers that come in the mail, the ones advertising records or magazines. Separate them along the perforated lines, and let your child stick them onto a plain piece of paper or use them to decorate her artwork.

Paper-Clip Jewelry

Paper clips

Show your child how to link paper clips together to form a necklace or bracelet. Use standard metal clips, bright plastic ones, or a combination of the two.

Magnet Magic

Refrigerator magnets
Heavy paper

Give your child a couple of refrigerator magnets and a piece of heavy paper. Place the paper between the two magnets and show your child how to move the top magnet by moving the bottom magnet. On the top side of the paper draw a road or some other pattern for your child to follow.

Lid Art

Plastic lids from gallon milk jugs
Glue
Paper plate or piece of cardboard

If you buy milk or juice in gallon plastic jugs, save the small plastic lids. Once you have a collection of different-colored lids, let your child glue them onto a piece of cardboard or a paper plate to create a design. Kids will also have fun sorting lids by color, lining them up end to end, creating patterns, or using them as play money.

Setting the Table

Plates
Silverware
Napkins
Glasses

When you aren't using your best china, have your child help
you set the table. Have her count the number of people who
will be eating, then count out the same number of knives,
forks, spoons, plates, napkins, and so on. Show her how to
place everything on the table properly. For younger children,
you may want to set the plates and other breakables yourself,
and have your child help you with silverware and napkins—
unless, of course, you are using paper plates!

I Love You Because . . .

Paper and pen
Crayons or markers

Ask your child, "Why do you love Daddy?" Write her responses on a sheet of plain or construction paper, and have your child decorate it with crayons or markers. Place the "love note" as a surprise in Dad's lunch the next day. You can vary the questions you ask your child, such as, "What's the funniest thing Daddy ever did?" Or do this for friends or grandparents and other relatives. Some of the answers you get may be priceless!

Little Carpenter

Golf tees
Styrofoam
Toy hammer

Give your child some golf tees, a toy hammer, and a piece of Styrofoam. She can hammer the golf tees into the foam in a design, or just hammer for the sake of hammering.

Memory

Index cards
Pen or marker

Sharpen your preschooler's memory skills by making your own memory game. Create two identical sets of index cards with letters of the alphabet, colors, shapes, or numbers. Start out with only a few, as this can be tough. Place all the cards, facedown, on the table. Have your child turn over one card, then put it back, facedown, on the table, and try to find the corresponding matching card. You can determine the number of tries allowed, and can make a game out of this between two or more children. At first your child may only guess, but it won't take long for her to get the idea. Begin the game with only a few cards, and add more as your child gets better; don't overwhelm her with too many cards at once.

Who Loves You?

Paper
Pen
Markers and/or stickers for decorating

Ask your child, "Who loves you?" and write down her answer.
Ask, "Who else loves you?" and write down each name, then
read her the list when she is finished. Top the list with the
title "Look Who Loves (child's name)" and let her decorate it
with markers or stickers. Stick it on the refrigerator or on her
bedroom wall to remind her how much she is loved.

Put Away the Silverware

Silverware
Utensil holder

Your child can help you put away the silverware as you remove
it from the dishwasher or drainer. Place your utensil holder on
the table with the clean utensils next to it. Your child can then
sort, count, and put them away.

Listening Game

Have your child close her eyes and guess the sounds you make. Use household objects, such as keys, coins, silverware, or a whistle. Tap on a pot with a spoon, snap your fingers, or click your tongue.

Newspaper Golf

Newspaper
Tape
Golf or tennis balls
Masking tape or paper

Make golf clubs for each player by rolling up several sheets of newspaper and taping them securely. Lay down a sheet of paper or use masking tape to mark several "holes" on the floor or carpet. Use your golf club to try to hit (roll) the ball to the hole. Reward the winner (the first to hit the ball to the hole) with a raisin, chocolate chip, or other small treat.

Sewing Practice

Heavy cardboard
Scissors
Hole punch
Shoelace or yarn
Tape (if using yarn)

Cut a shape out of heavy cardboard and punch holes around
the edges at regular intervals. Tie a knot in one end of an old
shoelace, or knot one end of a piece of yarn and wrap heavy
tape around the other end. Let your child sew by weaving the
shoelace through the punched holes. This fun activity is great
for hand/eye coordination.

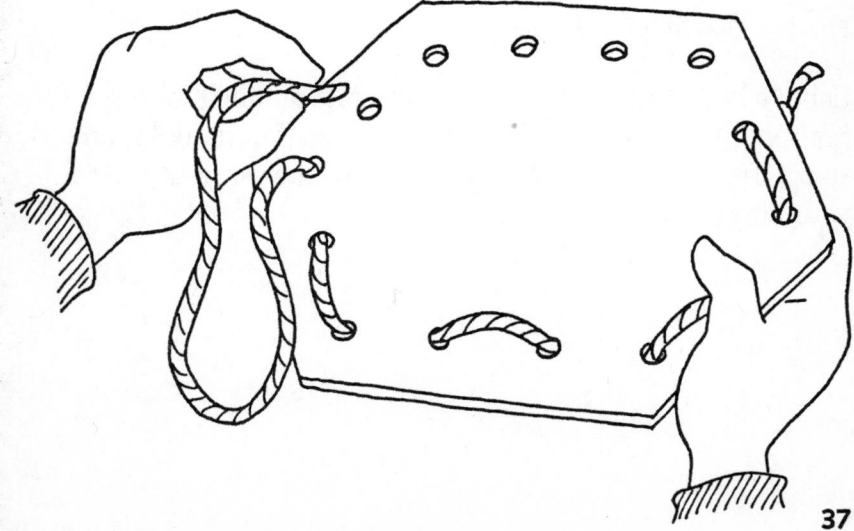

Hand Puppets

Washable markers

Using washable markers, draw a face on the palm of your child's hand, or draw small faces on the pads of each finger so that the puppets can "talk" to each other. Draw puppets on your own fingers and get some conversations going between your puppets and your child's.

Fun with Weights

Bathroom scale
Various household objects

Using a bathroom scale, weigh your child and help her weigh household objects: a stack of books, a bag of flour, dolls, and so on. Try to find something that weighs the same amount as your child.

Pillow Throw

If you have any breakables on tables or dressers, put them
away before trying this one!

Lots of throw pillows

Have one person sit on a bed or couch with the throw pillows.
Have the other person run across the room from one point to
another, while the person on the bed tries to hit the moving
target with the pillows.

Shape Shake

Cardboard
Scissors
String

Cut out a cardboard shape and pierce a small hole in the
center. Tie one end of a string to the doorknob of your child's
room and thread the opposite end of the string through the
shape's hole. Have your child stand across the room holding
and shaking the free end of the string. See how long it takes
her to shake the shape from one end to the other.

Doll Closet

Tension rod
Baby clothes hangers
Bookcase

Make a closet for all those little doll clothes by inserting a
tension rod across the lower shelf of a bookcase. Have your
child hang doll clothes onto baby clothes hangers and then
onto the rod. (Try to save some of your newborn-sized clothes,
bibs, and blankets; they are the perfect size for many dolls.)

Sorting Socks

Socks
Laundry basket

Take all the socks out of your child's sock drawer. Have her
identify each color as she puts them back. For some real fun,
give your child a laundry basket and have her collect all the
socks from every sock drawer in the house. She can amuse
herself for a long time sorting them by color, size, or owner. If
you like, separate the socks, mix them all up, and then have
your child find the matches for each sock. Keep in mind,
however, that you may have to rematch most of the socks
yourself after your child is done.

Sort the Laundry

Laundry

This is a great activity that will give your child some
household responsibility and teach a very practical skill at the
same time. Show your child how to sort the laundry before
you wash it. Even a very young child can separate whites,
colors, and darks, and it will save you time as well! You can
also have your child remove the clothes from the dryer, and
sort and carry them to the appropriate rooms when folded.
Folding may be a little tricky depending on your standards,
but you can let her tackle the easy things: towels, dishcloths,
baby blankets, and so on.

Hotter/Colder

Small toys or edible treats

Hide several household objects, small toys or edible treats
around the house and encourage your child to find them. Tell
her she is "hotter" when she is closer to the hidden item,
"colder" as she moves away from it.

Carpet Raceway

Books or scraps of wood
Matchbox cars or other toys with wheels

Make a raceway or train track on a carpet by laying down
books of equal thickness side by side to make a smooth lane,
or use pieces of plywood or two-by-fours. (Your raceway can be
any length and can be straight or have turns.) This will
transform the carpet into a smooth surface for racing toys
with wheels.

Living Room Picnic

Tablecloth
Picnic dishes
Picnic food
Summer clothing

Brighten the coldest, rainiest, or stormiest of days by having
an indoor picnic. Spread a tablecloth on the floor of your
living room and use outdoor dishes or paper plates. Picnic-
type dress (shorts or bathing suits) is essential, and don't
forget your sunglasses.

Indoor Camping

Sleeping bags
Marshmallows

Don't let the weather stop you from going camping; to a preschooler, indoor camping can be just as fun! Lay out the sleeping bags in front of the fireplace, if you have one. Eat marshmallows and sing campfire songs. Strum on a guitar if you can, and turn the night into a precious memory for you and your child.

Night at the Movies

Family video or favorite movie
Special snack

Whether your child watches a little television or a lot, you can still make an occasion of watching a special program or movie together. Snuggle under a blanket or lie on the floor. Dim the lights and have a special snack together.

Hide and Seek

Kitchen timer

Wind up your kitchen timer and hide it somewhere in the house. Have your child search for it by listening for its ticking sound.

Fishing

Construction paper
Scissors
Pen, crayon, or marker
Small box, pot, or other container

Cut fish shapes out of colored construction paper. On each fish write a different instruction: "Find something red"; "Count to ten"; "Touch your toes"; and so on. Place the fish in a small box or container and let your child pick one fish at a time. Read the instruction and have her perform it.

Tell Me a Story

Various household objects
Pillowcase or brown paper bag

Put five or six various household objects into a brown paper bag or pillowcase: keys, purse, stuffed animal, book, and so on. Remove each item from the bag one at a time, and create a story by adding one sentence for each item as it is removed: "Once upon a time there was a little white kitten named Angel. Angel just loved to read books, especially books about cookies."

Red Light/Green Light

Stand twenty to twenty-five feet away from your child. When you say "green light," have her walk, run, hop, skip, or crawl toward you. She must stop when you say "red light."

Balancing Board

Board measuring about 8 inches wide by 6 feet long
Magazines or books

Place a board across two piles of magazines or books (books will be less slippery than glossy magazines). Have your child practice keeping her balance by walking across the board. As your child grows more steady, you can place one end on a chair and she can walk up it, or place it across two chairs as she grows even more bold. Remember: The higher you build the balance beam, the more supervision your child will need.

Make a Tape

Tape recorder
Blank cassette tape

If you have access to a tape recorder, help your child make a tape for Dad to play on his way to work. Sing favorite songs, say nursery rhymes, tell him a story, talk about what you do when he's at work, tell him you love him and why you're thankful for him. This makes a great Father's Day gift. You can also use this idea for a grandparent or other special person.

Animal Charades

Variety of stuffed animals
Pillowcase

Place several stuffed animals in a pillowcase. Close your eyes while your child takes one out and looks at it. Have her put it back in the case and act out the animal, while you try to guess what it is.

Follow the Leader

Have your child follow you through the house, imitating the
sounds and movements you make. You can dance around,
pretend to be a bunny, a horse, a train, a car, and so on. Take
turns and let your child lead you.

Pretend Islands

Pillows

Place pillows on the carpet for pretend islands and imagine
the carpet is the ocean. Have your child jump from island to
island without falling in the water.

Bean Bag Toss

The Ziploc bag protects the beans even if the bag gets wet.

4-by-6-inch scraps of material
Needle and thread
Dried beans
Ziploc bag

Fill a small Ziploc bag with dried beans. Sew two squares of material together on three sides, leaving a space on the fourth side big enough to slide in the bag of beans. Turn the bag inside out to hide the seams, insert the bag of beans, then sew up the space. (If you don't have time to sew a bean bag, pour beans into an old sock, knot the open end, and turn down the cuff.) Use the bean bag to play catch, or have your child toss the bag into an empty laundry basket from a few feet away.

Shoe Trail

Empty laundry basket
Shoes

Give your child a laundry basket and have her fill it with shoes. Make a trail of shoes around the house, lining them up heel to toe. Follow the trail, counting as you go. Keep a list, and have your child count how many shoes each person has, or how many shoes of each color there are, or how many shoes there are in total. Help your child put the shoes away when she is done.

Indoor Treasure Hunt

Small toys or snacks
Treasure map (optional)

This is a great way to liven up a rainy day. Have an indoor treasure hunt by hiding several small toys, books, or special snacks around the house. Give your child clues or draw a map that leads to the treasure.

Go Fish

Stick for fishing pole
String
Magnet
Scissors
Construction paper
Glue or tape
Metal paper clips

Cut fish shapes out of construction paper. Glue or tape metal paper clips to the back of each fish. Make a fishing pole out of a long stick and a length of string. Tie a magnet on the end of the string. Go fishing. This works well if you place the "fish" on the floor and let your child dangle her line over the back of the couch. You can also use this game to help your child learn her basic skills: Draw a shape or write a letter or number on the back of each fish, and have her identify it when caught.

Play with Boxes

Cardboard boxes in various sizes

Your child can put supermarket boxes of all sizes to good use. She can make a train or a fort for herself or her animals, build a dollhouse, or create a car. You can be sure she will think of something new every time she plays with these boxes.

Whose Ear Is This?

Blindfold

For this activity you will need at least three people. Take turns blindfolding each other and trying to guess who each person is just by touching one feature: nose, finger, ear, hair, and so on.

Simon Says

This old favorite is a fun game to play with your child. Have your child follow your actions only when you say, "Simon says": "Simon says touch your toes"; "Simon says stretch your arms"; "Simon says jump up and down." Your child should remain motionless when you give a command that is not preceded by "Simon says." This is a lot of fun when done very quickly, and is a good game for a group. You can have each child sit down if she moves when she's not supposed to, and award a small prize to the last child who remains standing. Take turns being Simon.

CHAPTER 3
Kids in the Kitchen

"You cannot teach a child to take care of himself unless you let him try to take care of himself. He will make mistakes; and out of these mistakes will come his wisdom."
—*Francis Bacon*

Work and play are inseparable for kids; your work is very often your child's play. Whether you are in the kitchen a little or a lot, your child will naturally want to be with you. The kitchen is a tantalizing place for children, full of wonderful things to smell, touch, and taste. Anyone who has ever watched a small child eat will know that, to a child, food is as much a toy as it is a nourishment. Children, even as young as two, will enjoy making their own peanut butter sandwiches, and most will agree that finger Jell-O is one of the best foods ever invented! Make sure your child's hands are clean, accept that things may get a little messy, and let your child enjoy his food experience.

With a little bit of effort and a lot of patience on your part, the kitchen can also become a wonderful classroom for your child. Talk to him about the magic of the kitchen, how yeast or baking powder makes things rise, how the batter baked in the oven turns into a cake, or how cornstarch thickens a sauce. He will want to help you measure and mix, wash vegetables, cut out cookies, and sift dry ingredients. Include him in your work, and take the time to teach him as you cook.

Make or buy your child his own recipe box and fill it with his favorite recipes, written with simple words and illustrated with pictures and symbols. Include some simple "no-cook" recipes that he can make with little supervision. Consider providing your child with his very own Baker's Box (see page 3).

Remember to always be safety-conscious. Make sure any dangerous objects are well out of reach, and be sure to closely supervise any use of sharp utensils, the oven, or stove, or, better yet, make a rule that only an adult can use those things.

Fruit Kebabs

Small wooden skewers, Popsicle sticks, coffee stirrers, or
*   swizzle sticks*
Various fruit, cut into bite-sized pieces

Have your child create fruit kebabs by putting pieces of fruit
onto small wooden skewers, wooden Popsicle sticks, plastic
coffee stirrers, or swizzle sticks. As your child works, talk to
him about the different types of fruit, their colors, smells, and
tastes. Serve the kebabs for dessert or a tasty snack.

Mini Popsicles

Empty ice cube tray
Juice
Fruit (grapes, raisins, cherries)
Toothpicks

Fill an empty ice cube tray with juice, and put one or two
pieces of fruit (grapes, raisins, and cherries work well) and one
toothpick inside each compartment. Freeze and enjoy.

Taste Testing

Blindfold
Various food items

Blindfold your child and have him identify by taste and smell some of his favorite foods (ice cream, pickles, yogurt, cereal, cookies, and so on). Have him describe the different tastes and textures and ask him to group them as sweet, salty, bitter, sour, spicy, or tangy.

Flour Drawing

Cookie sheet
Flour

Lightly sprinkle the surface of a cookie sheet with flour. Show your child how to draw in it with his finger. Or draw a letter, number, or shape in the flour with your finger and have him draw the same next to yours.

Melon Bowl

Watermelon
Other melons (honeydew, cantaloupe)
Knife
Melon-ball scoop

Make a watermelon bowl by cutting a watermelon in half.
Have your child scoop out the melon with a melon-ball scoop.
Cut open several other melons and have your child continue
to make more melon balls. Fill the watermelon bowl with the
melon balls and serve as a summer dessert or tasty afternoon
snack.

Apple Shapes

Apples
Knife
Metal cookie cutters

Peel apples and cut them into thin slices. Give your child small metal cookie cutters and let him cut shapes out of the slices.

Homemade Peanut Butter

Peanuts in the shell
Food processor
Baby food jar (optional)
Decorative fabric and ribbon (optional)

Shelling enough peanuts to make a little peanut butter is sure to keep your child busy. Place the shelled peanuts in your food processor and grind until smooth. Store in a covered container. To give as a gift, place the peanut butter in a small baby food jar with lid. Cover the lid with a circle of fabric, and tie a ribbon around the neck of the jar to keep the fabric in place.

Pasta Play

Dried pasta
Bowls
Measuring cups
Mixing spoons

Give your child containers filled with various sizes and shapes
of dried pasta, such as macaroni, rotini, shells, and so on. Add
a few empty bowls, measuring cups, and a mixing spoon or
two, and let your child measure, mix, and match. If you like,
give your child string and let him make necklaces, bracelets,
ornaments, and other objects. (Supervise young children to
avoid strangulation.) As an option, dye the pasta using the
directions for pasta dye in Appendix A, Basic Craft Recipes. For
a variation, try using cereal, dried beans or rice in place of pasta.

Happy-Face Sandwich

Bread
Peanut butter
Raisins or chocolate chips
Knife

Spread peanut butter on one side of a piece of bread. Have your child decorate it with eyes, a nose, and a big, happy smile made of raisins or chocolate chips.

Banana Balls

Ripe bananas
Bowl
Fork
Finely chopped nuts
Cinnamon
Cookie sheet

Have your child mash a ripe banana in a bowl with a fork. Add finely chopped nuts and a dash of cinnamon, and mix. Form the mixture into small balls and place the balls on a cookie sheet. When all the balls are complete, cover the cookie sheet and refrigerate. These are great for a quick snack or for floating in cereal for breakfast.

Chase the Pepper

Pie plate or small sink
Pepper
Bar of soap
Sugar

Your child will love to show off this neat trick. Fill a pie plate or small sink with water. Shake pepper on the water and dip a piece of wet soap into it. The pepper will run away from the soap. Now shake some sugar into the clear area and the pepper will run back.

Aggression Cookies

This is truly one recipe your child can make all by himself.

Ingredients
3 cups quick-cooking oats
1½ cups brown sugar
1½ cups flour
1½ cups butter or margarine
1½ teaspoons baking powder

Materials
Large bowl
Cookie sheet

1. Dump all the ingredients into a large bowl and let your child really go at it! Pound, punch, and knead the batter—the longer and harder the dough is mixed, the better the cookies will taste!
2. When ready to bake, preheat the oven to 350 degrees.
3. Roll the dough into small balls and bake on an ungreased cookie sheet for 10 to 12 minutes.

Alphabet Cookies

This special vanilla dough handles like modeling clay, but also makes delicious cookies. Use this activity to strengthen your child's alphabet skills. The finished products make good place cards for birthday parties.

Ingredients
4½ cups unsifted all-purpose flour
1½ cups butter
3 hard-cooked egg yolks
¾ cup sugar
3 raw egg yolks
1½ teaspoons vanilla
Colored sugar or chocolate chips (optional)

Materials
Large bowl
Fork, knife
Cookie sheet

1. Measure flour into a large bowl.
2. Cut butter into small pieces and add to the flour. Mix with your fingers until the flour and butter form fine crumbs.
3. Mash cooked egg yolks with sugar and stir into the flour mixture.

4. Blend raw egg yolks with vanilla and stir into the flour mixture with a fork.
5. Press the mixture with your hands into a firm ball. Work with the dough at room temperature, but refrigerate it if you will bake it later.
6. Preheat the oven to 300 degrees.
7. Roll out the dough. Cut 3-inch or 4-inch strips and roll with your palm to make ropes.
8. Shape the ropes into letters. Flatten them slightly so they are about ¼-inch thick. If you like, decorate the letters with colored sugar or chocolate chips.
9. Place the letters on a cookie sheet and bake for 25 to 30 minutes.

Paintbox Cookies

These sturdy cookies, baked and glazed ahead, can be painted with food coloring for a rainy day or party project.

Ingredients
2 cups softened margarine or butter
2 cups granulated sugar
2 teaspoons vanilla
5 cups flour
5–9 teaspoons warm water
1½ pounds powdered sugar
Food coloring

Materials
Large bowl
Electric mixer or fork
Cookie sheet
Knife or cookie cutters
Aluminum foil
Paintbrush
Small cups

1. Beat butter, granulated sugar, and vanilla together.
2. Add flour and mix until thoroughly blended.
3. Preheat the oven to 300 degrees.

4. Roll out the dough on an ungreased cookie sheet to ¼–⅜-inch thickness. Cut into shapes with a knife or floured cookie cutters.

5. Bake for 25 to 30 minutes until dough is a pale golden color. Let cookies cool about 7 minutes, then transfer to a foil-covered surface.

6. To make icing, add warm water to icing sugar until icing is smooth and thick. Spread the icing onto the cookies, making a smooth surface. Let the icing dry thoroughly (8 to 24 hours).

7. When the icing is dry, paint on it with food coloring. Use a paintbrush and small cups of food coloring—undiluted for bright colors or slightly diluted for lighter ones. Food coloring will flow, so allow each color to dry briefly before adding the next.

Note: If making the cookies ahead of time, follow steps 1 to 6, and then store the cookies at room temperature for up to 4 days, or freeze for longer storage. Thaw before painting.

Cookie Cutouts

This is the tastiest rolled cookie recipe I've found.

Ingredients
2½ cups flour
1 teaspoon cinnamon
½ teaspoon ginger (optional)
½ teaspoon baking powder
¼ teaspoon baking soda
¼ teaspoon salt
¾ cup butter
½ cup liquid honey
⅓ cup granulated sugar
1 egg
Colored sugar or sprinkles
  (optional)

Materials
Medium bowl
Large bowl
Electric mixer or fork
Rolling pin
Cookie cutters
Cookie sheet

1. Stir together flour, cinnamon, ginger, baking powder,
   baking soda, and salt in a medium bowl. Set aside.
2. In a large bowl, cream together butter, honey, and sugar
   until smooth.
3. Beat in egg.
4. Stir in flour mixture, mixing well. Cover and refrigerate
   dough for 1½ hours or until firm enough to roll and cut.
5. Preheat the oven to 350 degrees.

6. Roll out the dough on a well-floured surface, about one-third of the dough at a time. Cut into desired shapes using floured cookie cutters.
7. Place on a lightly greased cookie sheet. Bake for 8 to 10 minutes until lightly browned and firm to the touch. Makes 3 to 4 dozen cookies.

Note: You can decorate these with colored sugar or sprinkles before baking, or, when cool, cover with icing and then decorate.

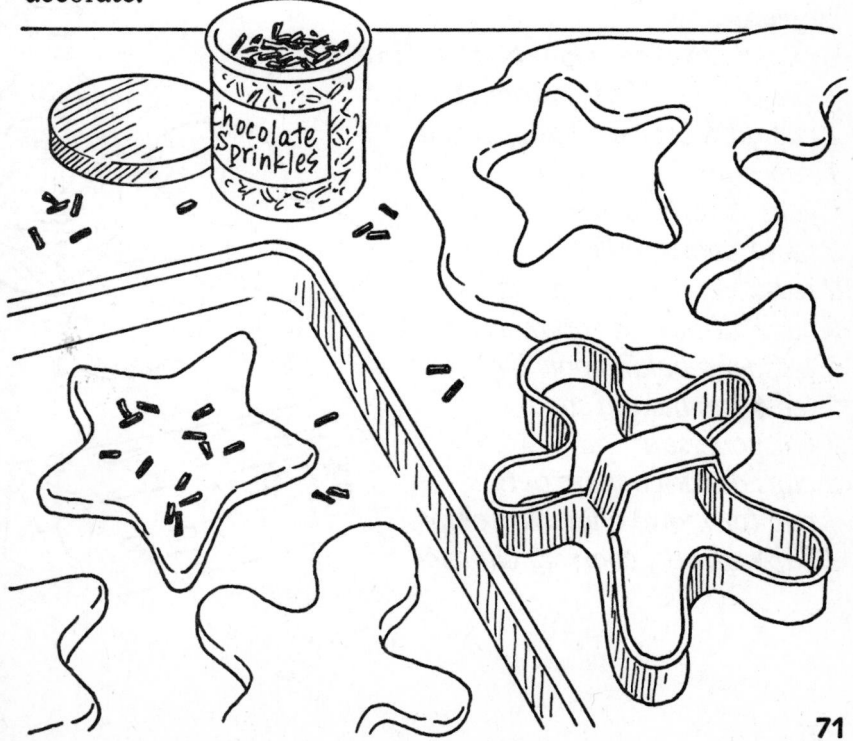

Best Chocolate Chip Cookies in the World

This makes a truly great chocolate chip cookie. Be sure to refrigerate the dough before baking, and don't overbake them; they harden as they cool. Double the batch and freeze half of the dough for instant, no-mess baking fun on a rainy day.

Ingredients

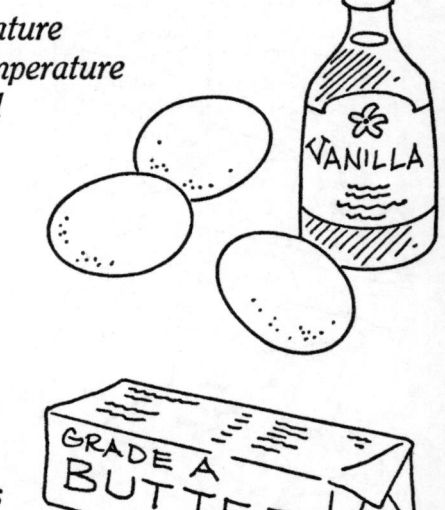

½ cup margarine, room temperature
½ cup unsalted butter, room temperature
1 cup dark brown sugar, packed
1 cup granulated sugar
2 eggs, lightly beaten
2 tablespoons milk
2 teaspoon vanilla extract
2 cups all-purpose flour, sifted
1 teaspoon baking powder
1 teaspoon baking soda
1 teaspoon salt
2 cups quick-cooking oats
1 cup (or more) chocolate chips
1 cup walnuts, coarsely chopped

Materials
Large bowl
Electric mixer
Spoon for mixing
Cookie sheet
Teaspoon or tablespoon
Wire racks

1. Cream the margarine, butter, and both sugars in a large bowl until light and fluffy.
2. Add the eggs, milk, and vanilla and beat until blended.
3. Sift the flour, baking powder, baking soda, and salt together and add to the butter mixture. Stir just until blended.
4. Stir in the oats. Fold in the chocolate chips and walnuts.
5. Cover the dough and refrigerate for at least one hour.
6. Preheat the oven to 350 degrees. Grease the cookie sheet.
7. Shape the dough into balls, using a rounded teaspoon for small cookies or a scant tablespoon for large. Flatten slightly into rounded disks. Place 2 inches apart on the cookie sheet.
8. Bake until the edges are slightly browned, but the cookies are still white, 8 to 10 minutes. Remove from the oven and let cool for 5 minutes. Transfer to wire racks to cool completely.

Animal Pancakes

Ingredients

1¼ cups all-purpose flour
2 tablespoons sugar
2 teaspoons baking powder
¾ teaspoon salt
3 tablespoons salad oil
1⅓ cups milk
1 egg, slightly beaten
Chocolate chips or blueberries
  (optional)

Materials

Large bowl
Fork, spoon
Electric griddle or skillet

1. In a large bowl, with fork, mix flour, sugar, baking powder, and salt; add salad oil, milk, and egg, and stir just until the flour mixture is moistened.
2. Preheat an electric griddle or a skillet; grease lightly with salad oil.
3. Use a spoon to drop the batter into the pan to make animal shapes. A bunny needs only a round shape for the head and two long shapes for ears (and maybe chocolate chips or blueberries for eyes). Try to make a mouse with an oval body, smaller drops for the head, ears, and feet, and a long thin tail. A turtle can be one big spoonful of batter surrounded by six smaller drops. Try a cat, bird, giraffe, elephant—use your imagination!

Snow-Topped Cupcakes

Ingredients
1 egg
1 cup milk
1 teaspoon vanilla
1¼ cup white sugar
½ cup margarine, melted

1¾ cup flour
2½ teaspoons baking powder
½ teaspoon salt
White frosting
Shredded coconut

Materials
Large bowl
Electric mixer
Paper-lined muffin tins

1. Preheat the oven to 350 degrees.
2. Combine egg, milk, vanilla, sugar, and margarine in a large bowl and blend on medium speed with electric mixer.
3. Add flour, baking powder, and salt, and mix on the top speed of mixer for 2 minutes.
4. Pour into paper-lined muffin tins. Bake for 20 minutes.
5. Let your child frost the cupcakes with white frosting and dip them in coconut for snow. Serve them for dinner or a teddy-bear tea.

Peanut Butter Oat Squares

These are delicious for adults and children alike!

Ingredients
½ cup butter, softened
1 cup brown sugar, lightly packed
½ cup corn syrup
1 teaspoon salt
2 teaspoons vanilla
4 cups quick-cooking oats
½ cup peanut butter
½ cup chocolate chips
1½ teaspoons butter

Materials
Large bowl
Fork for mixing
9-by-13-inch baking
  pan, greased
Small saucepan
Teaspoon, knife

1. Preheat the oven to 350 degrees.
2. Cream butter and brown sugar in a large bowl.
3. Add corn syrup, salt, vanilla, and oats. Mix well.
4. Spread mixture evenly in a greased baking pan. Bake for 15 minutes. Cool slightly.
5. Spread peanut butter evenly over top.
6. Combine chocolate chips and butter in a small saucepan, and melt until smooth. Drizzle over the peanut butter, or dot onto the peanut butter with a teaspoon and use the point of a knife to swirl the chocolate.
7. Cool until the chocolate sets, then cut into squares.

Fantastic Fudge Brownies

Ingredients

Dough:
2 cups sugar
4 heaping tablespoons cocoa
1 cup butter
4 eggs, beaten
1 teaspoon vanilla
1 cup flour
1 cup walnuts, chopped

Icing:
2 cups powdered sugar
2 tablespoons butter
2 tablespoons cocoa
2 tablespoons boiling water
2 teaspoons vanilla

Materials

Large bowl, medium bowl
Electric mixer
9-by-13-inch baking pan, greased

1. Preheat the oven to 350 degrees. Grease the baking pan.
2. Cream sugar, cocoa, and butter in a large bowl.
3. Add beaten eggs and vanilla. Then add flour and walnuts.
4. Bake in a greased baking pan for 30 minutes. The top will appear to be underdone (falls in the middle), but don't overcook. These brownies should be moist and chewy.
5. While the brownies are baking, mix all the icing ingredients together in a medium bowl with an electric mixer.
6. Ice the brownies immediately after removing from oven so the icing will melt into a shiny glaze.

Chocolate Pizza Pie

Ingredients
1¾ cup semisweet chocolate chips, divided
½ cup + 2 tablespoons golden flavor shortening
½ cup all-purpose flour
½ cup granulated sugar
2 eggs
1 teaspoon baking powder
2 tablespoons water
Assorted candy for decoration

Materials
Double boiler
12-inch pizza pan
Small bowl

1. Preheat the oven to 375 degrees.
2. Melt 1 cup chocolate chips and ½ cup shortening in a double boiler; cool.
3. Add flour, sugar, eggs, and baking powder; mix well.
4. Spread evenly onto a well-greased 12-inch pizza pan.
5. Bake for 15 minutes. Cool.
6. Combine ¾ cup chocolate chips, 2 tablespoons of shortening, and 2 tablespoons of water in a double boiler; melt, then stir to combine.
7. Spread glaze over cooled pizza. Decorate with candies.

Peanut Butter Cups

This is a very easy and tasty recipe that kids can make themselves with a little help.

Ingredients
1½ cups Rice Krispies
1 cup carob or chocolate chips
1 cup peanut butter

Materials
Wax paper
Double boiler
12 muffin cups

1. Roll the rice cereal between wax paper until it is a powdery texture.
2. Melt the carob or chocolate chips in a double boiler; remove from heat.
3. Add the peanut butter and cereal powder. Mix well.
4. Divide the mixture evenly among the muffin cups, smooth the surface, and cool in the refrigerator to harden. You may want to line the muffin cups with aluminum foil, or spray them with vegetable spray so the cups will come out easier. However, do not use paper liners, as the paper will absorb the oil from the peanut butter.

Crunch and Munch

This is a wonderful snack to munch on as you watch your favorite movie, television show, or home video together. But be warned—it's addictive!

Ingredients
½ cup butter or margarine, melted
½ cup honey
1 cup peanuts or other nuts, chopped
12 cups popped popcorn

Materials
Small saucepan
Cookie sheet

1. Preheat the oven to 350 degrees.
2. Combine melted butter or margarine and honey in a small saucepan; heat until well-blended. Add chopped nuts.
3. Pour over the popcorn and mix well.
4. Spread the popcorn mixture in a thin layer on a cookie sheet and bake for 12 minutes, until crisp. Stir often to avoid burning.

Popcorn Ball Creatures

Ingredients

¾ cup sugar
1 teaspoon white vinegar
¾ cup brown sugar
½ cup light corn syrup

½ cup water
¼ teaspoon salt
¾ cup butter
8 cups popped popcorn

Materials

Medium saucepan
Candy thermometer
Large bowl
Wax paper

1. Stir all ingredients except popcorn and butter in a medium saucepan over medium heat until the mixture reaches 260 degrees on a candy thermometer (hard ball stage).
2. Reduce temperature to low; add butter.
3. Put popcorn in a large bowl. Pour the mixture over it, coating the popcorn. Cool slightly.
4. Butter your child's hands and let him mold the popcorn into animal shapes. Place the shapes on wax paper until ready to eat.

Rice Krispie Pops

A new way to serve an old favorite!

Ingredients
¼ cup margarine or butter
4 cups miniature, or 40 regular, marshmallows
5 cups Rice Krispies

Materials
3-quart saucepan
Popsicle sticks

1. Melt margarine in a saucepan, then add marshmallows and cook over low heat, stirring constantly, until syrupy.
2. Remove from heat, add cereal, and stir until well coated.
3. Shape the mixture into an oval around a wooden Popsicle stick.

To make Rice Krispie Tarts: Prepare recipe as above. Add cereal and stir until well coated. Press the mixture into a buttered muffin tin to form a tart shell; fill with fresh fruit or ice cream.

Popsicles

Ingredients
1 package Kool-Aid
1 package Jell-O
1¼ cups sugar
¾ cup hot water
¾ cup cold water

Materials
2 bowls
Popsicle molds

1. Mix the dry ingredients thoroughly in a bowl.
2. Measure 6 tablespoons of the dry ingredients into a another bowl; add the hot and cold water.
3. Pour into Popsicle molds and freeze.
4. Store the remaining dry ingredients in an airtight container for future use.

Lollipops

Ingredients
¼ cup butter
¾ cup sugar
½ cup light corn syrup
Food coloring

Materials
16 Popsicle sticks
Cookie sheet, buttered
Medium saucepan
Candy thermometer
Tablespoon
Plastic wrap

1. Evenly space 16 Popsicle sticks on a buttered cookie sheet.
2. In a saucepan, heat butter, sugar, and corn syrup over medium-high heat; stir until it boils. Reduce heat to medium. Cook until mixture reaches 270 degrees on a candy thermometer, stirring often.
3. Add food coloring.
4. Drop the mixture by tablespoon onto the end of each Popsicle stick. Cool.
5. When the lollipops are cool, take them off the cookie sheet and wrap them in plastic wrap.

Finger Jell-O

The following Finger Jell-O recipes make use of different ingredients, but give basically the same result. Use the recipe that best suits the ingredients you have on hand or prefer to use.

Gelatin/Jell-O Recipe
This recipe uses a combination of unflavored gelatin and commercial Jell-O.

Ingredients
2 envelopes unflavored gelatin
6-ounce package Jell-O
2½ cups cold water, divided

Materials
Small bowl
Medium saucepan
Baking pan, lightly greased
Cookie cutters or knife

1. Dissolve unflavored gelatin in a small bowl with 1 cup cold water. Set aside.
2. In a medium saucepan, bring 1 cup of water to a boil and add Jell-O. Bring to a boil again and remove from heat.

3. Add gelatin mixture. Stir and add ½ cup cold water.
4. Pour into a lightly greased baking pan and set in refrigerator until solid (2 hours).
5. Use cookie cutters or a sharp knife to cut into shapes.

Gelatin/Juice Recipe
Avoid using commercial Jell-O by trying this recipe.

Ingredients
3 envelopes unflavored gelatin
1 12-ounce can frozen juice concentrate, thawed
12 ounces water
Sugar (optional)

Materials
Medium saucepan
Baking pan, lightly greased
Cookie cutters or knife

1. In a medium saucepan, soften gelatin in thawed juice concentrate; bring the water to a boil.
2. Add the juice/gelatin mixture to the boiling water and stir until gelatin is dissolved. Add sugar for extra sweetening, if desired.
3. Pour into a lightly greased baking pan and set in refrigerator until solid (2 hours).

CHAPTER 4
Outdoor Adventures

"Any adult who spends even fifteen minutes with a child outdoors finds himself drawn back to his own childhood, like Alice falling down the rabbit hole."
—*Sharon MacLatchie*

Children of all ages have such an endless amount of energy. Outdoor play, every day, in almost any weather, is essential. Most children are as happy all bundled up for the snow as they are in shorts in the summertime. Rain provides countless opportunities for play, whether walking beneath an umbrella or stomping in the puddles, and a brisk walk is appropriate almost anytime. Playing outdoors in all types of weather is great fun for kids. You should encourage your child's outdoor play every day, and join her whenever you can.

The following suggestions will provide your preschooler with some fun and interesting things to do outdoors. Most activities require a minimum of materials, and you will find that by making slight adaptations, most are suitable for any season and any weather.

Sidewalk Drawing

Chalk

Have your child use white or colored chalk to draw on the sidewalk. Teach her how to play games, such as tick-tack-toe or hangman, or simply let her create masterpieces to her heart's content. The "paper" will always be big enough for whatever project she undertakes, and you won't have to worry about display or storage space when she is done! Special sidewalk chalk is available, but regular chalk will do—just be sure to have lots, as it wears down pretty quickly. Also make sure to limit your child's creativity to your residence's sidewalk, unless you ask the neighbors' permission first.

Bubble Pipe

Paper cup
Straw
Dish detergent
Water
Food coloring

Help your child make this simple bubble pipe. Poke a pencil hole on the side of a paper cup, one inch from the bottom, and stick a drinking straw through it, halfway into the cup. Pour dish detergent into the cup until the straw is covered. Add a little water and a few drops of food coloring. Blow gently until beautiful colored bubbles froth over the rim of the cup and fill the air.

Bubble Solution

2 cups warm water
1 cup liquid dishwashing soap
¼ cup glycerin
1 teaspoon sugar
Funnel, straws, six-pack plastic beverage holders, or other
unbreakable household objects

Mix together water, dishwashing soap, glycerin, and sugar. Use various unbreakable objects found around the house to blow spectacular bubbles: funnels, straws, six-pack beverage holders. Dip the objects in the bubble solution and blow through them, or wave them through the air like wands. Store the bubble solution in a plastic container with a tight-fitting lid.

Paint the House

Paintbrush
Bucket of water
Painter's cap

Give your child a clean paintbrush, a bucket full of water, and a painter's cap and let her paint the outside of the house, the car, or the sidewalk. Not only will your child feel proud of doing grown-up stuff, she will actually do something useful in the process, and get fresh air and exercise in addition. If your child is old enough to think that painting with water is silly, put some soap into the water and tell her she is washing the house. (In this case, you may not want her to wash the car; it could result in soap streaks.)

Sandpaper Play

Sandpaper
Wood scraps
Glue (optional)
Paint or markers (optional)

Give your child a piece of sandpaper and some small wood scraps. Show her how to sand the wood, and talk about the difference between rough and well-sanded textures. Sanded scraps of wood can be glued together to create wood sculptures and painted or decorated with markers. To avoid splinters, you may want your child to wear gloves for this activity.

Mining for Gold

Small rocks
Gold or silver spray paint

Spray some small rocks with gold or silver spray paint to resemble gold or silver nuggets. Bury the nuggets in the dirt in your yard or sandbox, give your child a shovel, and have her dig for buried treasure. Give younger children some directions, like cold or hot, so they don't get too frustrated. Give older children a treasure map to follow.

Backyard Camping

Tent
Sleeping bags
Pillows
Flashlight
Snack

You don't have to go far to give your preschooler the outdoor experience. On a fine summer night, set up your tent in the backyard. For children, there is something almost magical about walking in the dark, so go for a walk: listen to night noises and look at stars. If a backyard bonfire is not allowed in your neighborhood, have a snack and a sing-along by the light of a flashlight before you pile into your sleeping bags for the night.

If your child is too scared to spend a whole night outdoors, limit the activity to the walk, and then pile into the house for hot cocoa.

Obstacle Course

Miscellaneous outdoor objects

Use a variety of outdoor objects to create an obstacle course
for your child to run around. Have her run around one way,
then have her do the course in reverse. You can time her, or
she can race with siblings and friends. Do not use objects that
have sharp corners or that can tip over easily. If necessary,
cushion objects with pillows and blankets.

Backyard Picnic

Blanket
Picnic food
Outdoor toys

You don't have to trek to the park to have a picnic. Set up a
picnic in your own backyard: Spread out a blanket, set up the
goodies, and bring out the balls and other outdoor toys to
complete the fun. In warmer weather, turn on the sprinkler or
fill the kiddy pool for some water play.

Hopscotch

Hopscotch grid
Marker

Hopscotch is a good game for counting, coordination, balance, and improving physical agility (and it's a lot of fun, too). Look for a hopscotch grid at the local schoolyard or draw one on your sidewalk with chalk. Give your child a marker (a small chain works well as a marker), show her how to throw it onto each consecutively numbered square, and have her hop on one foot to the end of the grid and back again, being careful not to hop in the square where the marker lays.

Watch the Sunset

Blanket
Snack

On a warm summer night, take a blanket and a special snack and go to a place where you can watch the sunset. You may want to bring crayons or colored pencils and a pad of paper and have your child try to capture the colors of the sunset in a drawing. If your child is too young to draw a sunset, have her find colored pencils or crayons to match the colors of the sky.

Mud Painting

Paintbrush
Mud

In a bucket or other container, mix water with some clean dirt or earth (without stones, grass, glass, or any other particles); keep the mud thin. Give your child a paintbrush and have her dip it into the mud and draw pictures or write words on the sidewalk. Be prepared: She will most likely use herself as a canvas as well! Your child will have fun hosing her creations off later, or you can leave them for the next rainfall.

Ice Blocks

Water
Tempera paint
Cardboard milk cartons

Mix tempera paint with water, pour into cardboard milk cartons, and freeze to make large, colorful ice blocks. You can freeze them outside if the weather is cold enough, or use your freezer if you have room. (If you like, make smaller blocks by freezing colored water in clean plastic food containers or ice cube trays.) Show your child how to build a wall by sticking the blocks together with water. The wall will last a long time if placed outside, out of direct sunlight, and temperatures remain below freezing.

Wash the Dishes

Baby bathtub or large basin
Water
Miscellaneous nonbreakable household items
Child's toys and play dishes
Soap (optional)

On a warm day, set a tub of water on the deck or in the backyard and fill it with plastic cups, funnels, straws, sponges, sieves, and so on. For more fun, add a little soap. Dress your child in a bathing suit and have her wash her toys or dishes.

Quiet Time

Blanket
Books
Pillows (optional)

After lunch on a hot summer day, spread out your blanket in a shady spot under a tree. Take your child's favorite books and toys, something cool to drink, and maybe a pillow. Read, play, tell stories, or simply take a leisurely nap—both of you!

Slip and Slide

Garbage bags or a large sheet of plastic
Liquid dishwashing detergent
Hose or sprinkler

This is great fun for a hot day. Spread out a large sheet of
plastic or a few plastic garbage bags that have been cut open
to lie flat. Pour a little bit of liquid dishwashing detergent on
the plastic, then turn the hose or sprinkler on it. Your kids
will have great fun getting a running start then sliding on the
plastic. This works great at the foot of a slide or on a gentle
slope. Make sure to remove any rocks or other sharp objects
from under the plastic.

Kickball

All the balls you can find

Gather together all the balls you can find in your house:
tennis balls, soccer balls, basketballs, beach balls, and so on.
Line them up one foot apart and have your child kick each
one. See which one is the easiest to kick, which one goes the
farthest, which one goes the highest, and so on.

Mud Pie

Sand
Dirt
Water
Bucket
Cake pan or pie plate
Grass or flower petals for decoration

Make some really good mud for your child's play. Hand-mix sand, clean dirt, and water in a large bucket. Keep the mud really thick. Give your child a cake pan or pie plate and let her make a pie. Decorate the results of your child's efforts with grass or flower petals and bake in the sun.

Water Fight

Water balloons, water pistols, garden hose, or tub or pool of water and plastic containers

Using water balloons, water pistols, a garden hose, or a big tub or pool of water and some plastic containers, have a water fight with your child. Invite some of your child's friends over for the fun, and serve Popsicles or ice-cream cones afterward.

Nature Walk

Notebook
Pen or pencil
Bird book (optional)

Take a nature walk with your child. Try to notice as many different types of trees, bugs, and birds as you can. Keep a list of what you see. If you like, bring colored pencils and let your child draw the things she observes. If you can't identify a bug, tree, or bird, or if your child asks questions you can't answer, write down the item's description and your child's questions to look up on your next trip to the library.

101

Berry Picking

Sunscreen
Sun hat
Bag lunch
Juice
Books

Every child should pick berries at least once in her life! Kids find strawberries the easiest to pick, as they are low to the ground, easy to see, and have no thorns. Find a farm that allows you to pick your own fruit. Go early in the day before it gets too hot, and don't forget the sunscreen and a sun hat. Most preschoolers won't last more than half an hour at this, so take lunch, juice, and some books for your child to enjoy in the shade when she tires. At home, have your child help you wash and hull the berries. Homemade jam is a marvelous project if you are feeling ambitious.

CHAPTER 5
Out and About

"I suppose there must be in every mother's life the inevitable moment when she has to take two small children shopping in one big store."
—*Shirley Jackson*

Children just naturally have the desire and the energy to play all the time, but there are times when your child will just have to sit. It may be a long ride in the car, or at the doctor's, dentist's or hairdresser's, or while you wait for your meal to arrive in a restaurant. Consider providing your child with his very own take-along Busy Bag (see page 5). No matter where you are or what you do, be prepared with quick, easy activities that require a minimum of props to keep a cranky child busy and calm, and a parent sane.

Add-On Stories

This is a good game at the dinner table or in the car. One person starts a story and each person takes a turn continuing it. You may want to have each person add a sentence, or choose a "pointer" to conduct the story. The pointer decides who goes next and can stop a person at any time, even in midsentence. You may want to choose a topic or theme for your story, or leave it completely open and see what kind of nonsense results.

Fun with Words

Ask your child to tell you what certain words mean to him. Pick out everyday words that he has likely heard before. Some suggestions to get you started: concrete, marriage, retire, divorce, bachelor, anniversary, occasion, special, obedient, country. You may be surprised to find that some of the words in your child's vocabulary are something of a mystery to him. Some of the answers you get will be priceless; write them down for posterity!

What Am I?

Make up riddles about animals, objects, or people for your child to solve. For an elephant you could say, "I am very large; I have a long trunk; I live in Africa. What am I?" For a fire truck, you may say, "I am big and red; I have a loud siren; I help put out fires. What am I?" Describe people by what they do (doctors, nurses, police officers), or friends and family by how they look (tall, wears glasses, long hair). Be specific to help your child solve the riddle without getting too frustrated.

Beep

Choose a familiar story, song, or rhyme that your child has heard often. Read or recite the story, song, or rhyme, but substitute wrong words or names in obvious places. For example: "Old MacDonald had a car" or "Mary had a little dog." Have your child listen for the incorrect words and say "Beep!" when he hears one.

Silly Questions

Ask your child silly questions to help him use his imagination and make choices. For example: "Would you rather be a bird or a cow? Why?" or "Would you rather be a table or a chair? Why?" Take turns asking the questions and giving the answers.

Guessing Bag

Pillowcase or drawstring bag
Small, unbreakable household objects

Place a variety of small, unbreakable household objects inside a bag. Close the bag so the objects are not visible. Have your child feel the objects through the bag and guess what they are.

Felt Doll

Felt
Pen or marker
Cardboard
Glue
Scissors
Scraps of yarn and fabric
Shoe box

Draw the shape of a person on a square of felt. The person should have clearly defined arms and legs, with the arms held away from the body. Glue the felt to a piece of cardboard and cut out the doll. Glue on yarn for hair, and draw a face with a marker. To make clothing for the doll, place the doll on scraps of fabric and use a marker to trace around the body. Cut out the clothes and dress the doll; the cloth will stick to the doll's felt body. Store the doll and clothes in a shoebox and take the box with you on long car rides.

Magnet Fun

Refrigerator magnets, magnet-backed letters, and numbers
Cookie sheet or cake pan

This activity will help keep your little ones busy in the car when going on long trips. Bring along all the magnetic-backed toys you can find, including refrigerator magnets, magnet-backed letters, numbers, and so on. Your child can use the magnets to spell words or create pictures on the cookie sheet or cake pan.

Something Blue

Look around you as you wait in a doctor's office or a restaurant, or as you drive in the car. Have your child name five things that are blue, red, yellow, and so on.

Edible Necklace

Shoestring licorice
Cereal or crackers with holes in the middle

Tie a knot at one end of a piece of shoestring licorice (or a plain piece of string). Show your child how to thread cereal or crackers with holes in them on the string, and then tie both ends together into a knot. The end result will amuse your child for quite some time. In the grocery store, he can eat one piece each time you put something in the cart; in the car, he can eat one piece each time he sees a dog or a red car.

Portable Flannel Board

Shoe box
Felt
Flannel scraps
Scissors

Cover the top of a shoe box with felt to make a small flannel board. Cut colored flannel scraps into various sizes and shapes, such as animals, cars, people, circles, squares, or triangles, or try letters and numbers if you feel ambitious. Store the pieces in the box and take it along on your next car trip. Your child can form designs or words on the top of the shoe box using the cut-out pieces.

CHAPTER 6

Reading, Writing, 'Rithmetic, and More

" ... children must be ready to learn from the first day of school. And of course, preparing children for school is a historic responsibility of parents."
—*George Bush*

Parents have few responsibilities more important or more rewarding than helping their child to learn. As a parent, you are your child's first and most important teacher. Children generally learn what adults around them value, and you can use your daily activities to informally teach your children about reading, math, geography, and science, among other things. Children are naturally curious, and there is much you can do to advance their knowledge in these academic areas. The activities in this chapter will help you provide opportunities for your child to understand the connection between academic knowledge and the skills you use every day at home and at work.

READING READINESS

During the preschool years, children develop at an extra-ordinary rate. Each day's experiences, however familiar to adults, can be fresh and exciting to curious preschoolers. Although your child's incessant curiosity may be aggravating, especially at the end of a long day, it provides an opportunity for you to help her connect daily experiences with words. Tying language to the world your child knows allows her to go beyond that world to explore new ideas. Not only do parents have abundant opportunities to help children develop language, but these opportunities often occur naturally and easily.

While connecting experience to language is an important foundation for learning to read, no activity is more important for preparing your child to succeed as a reader than reading aloud together. When you read to your children, they almost automatically learn about written language. They learn that the words in a particular written story are always in the same order and on the same page. They may also learn that print goes from left to right, that words are made up of letters, that each letter has at least two forms (capital and small) and that there are spaces between words.

Take your child to the library on a regular basis. (Our children receive their very own library cards when they can print their name.) Help your child find her way around the library, and show her how to look for books by her (or your) favorite authors. Appendix D provides a list of some of the best read-aloud books for young children. I also recommend *The Read-Aloud Handbook* by Jim Trelease (4th edition, Penguin Books, 1995), or *Honey for a Child's Heart* by Gladys Hunt (3rd edition, Zondervan, 1989). These books offer lots of great reading suggestions for children of all ages.

While reading with your child, you will often have opportunities to answer her questions about the names, sounds, and shapes of letters. Preschoolers are very observant and often focus on company trademarks and logos that include or resemble letters of the alphabet. For example, the golden arches at McDonald's look like an M; pointing that out may be an easy way to begin. Television programs like *Sesame Street* also may help your child learn letters and the sounds they represent. Try to watch these shows with your child so you can talk to her about the letters on the screen and point out all the other places those letters appear.

Research has shown that children who know the names and sounds of letters when they enter school learn to read sooner. The following activities will help your preschooler learn to identify letters, sounds, and words.

Alphabet Puzzle

Index cards
Pen or markers
Scissors

Print a capital letter on the left side of an index card and the corresponding lowercase letter on the right. Cut each card into two parts with a wavy or zigzag line to make two puzzle pieces. Mix all the puzzle pieces and have your child put them together again.

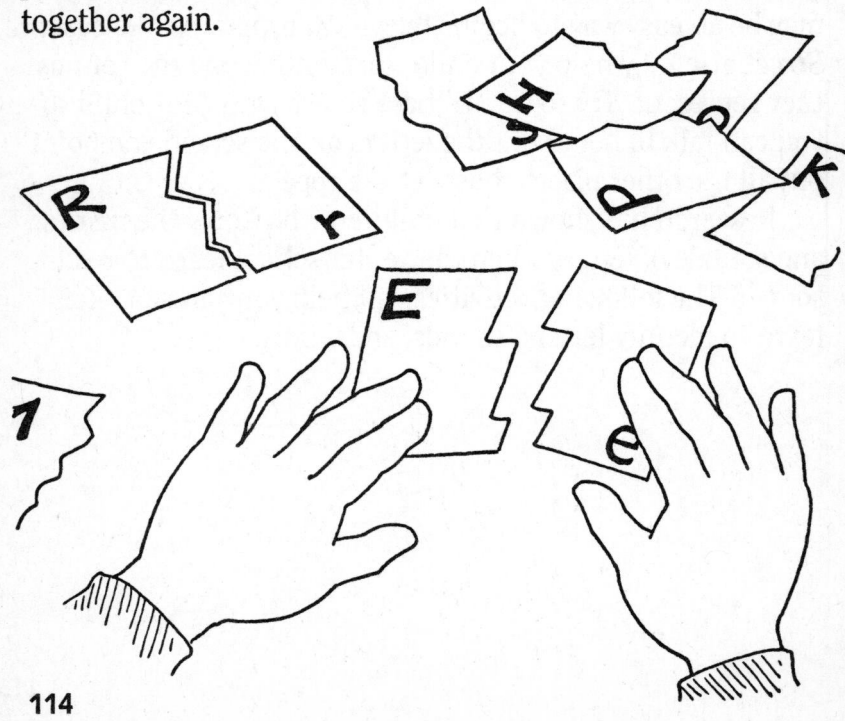

Alphabet Playdough

Playdough or modeling clay (see Appendix A)

Help your child form letters out of playdough or modeling clay. Then, have her close her eyes, feel a letter, and try to identify it by shape. As a tasty variation, make some Alphabet Cookies (see Chapter 3) and bake your alphabet!

Alphabet Match-Up

Clothespins
Paper
Tape
Pen or marker
Old magazines
Scissors

Write the letters of the alphabet on small pieces of paper and tape them to clothespins, or print the letters right on the clothespins. Cut out magazine pictures, one for each letter of the alphabet, and have your child match the clothespin letters to the beginning sounds of the objects in the pictures. Clip the clothespins to the corresponding pictures.

Dictionary Zoo

There is a delightful book called *Alfred's Alphabet Walk* by Victoria Chess (Greenwillow Books, 1979) that would nicely complement this activity.

Small notebook or loose sheets of paper
Crayons or markers
Old magazines
Scissors
Glue

This is a good rainy day project that can be completed during one or more sittings. Help your child print a letter of the alphabet on each page of a small notebook, or use loose sheets of plain or colored paper. Have your child draw a picture of an animal that begins with that letter, or cut animal pictures from old magazines and glue them onto each page.

Alphabet Book

Small notebook or loose sheets of paper
Crayons or markers
Old magazines
Scissors
Glue
Photos of friends and family (optional)

This is a long-term project that is great for rainy afternoons. Help your child print a letter of the alphabet on each page of a small notebook, or use loose sheets of plain or colored paper. Your child can draw a picture of something that begins with that letter, cut pictures from old magazines and glue them onto each page, or use photographs of friends and family members.

Find the Letter

Paper
Scissors
Pen or marker
3 plastic cups or coffee/tea mugs

Cut out circles of paper small enough to hide beneath a cup or a mug. Write different letters on each circle. Place three tea or coffee cups on the table and hide a paper circle under only one of them. Have your child guess where the letter is and identify the letter when she finds it. Take turns hiding the circles.

Connect the Dots

Paper
Pen or marker
Crayon

Draw a large dot-to-dot outline of your child's name on paper. Have her use a crayon to connect the dots to spell her name.

Connect-the-Dot Alphabet

Paper
Pen, marker, or crayon

Draw a dot-to-dot outline of a simple picture. (Try tracing some pictures from your child's coloring books.) Starting with the letter A, place each letter of the alphabet at a consecutive dot. Have your child connect the dots by identifying each letter.

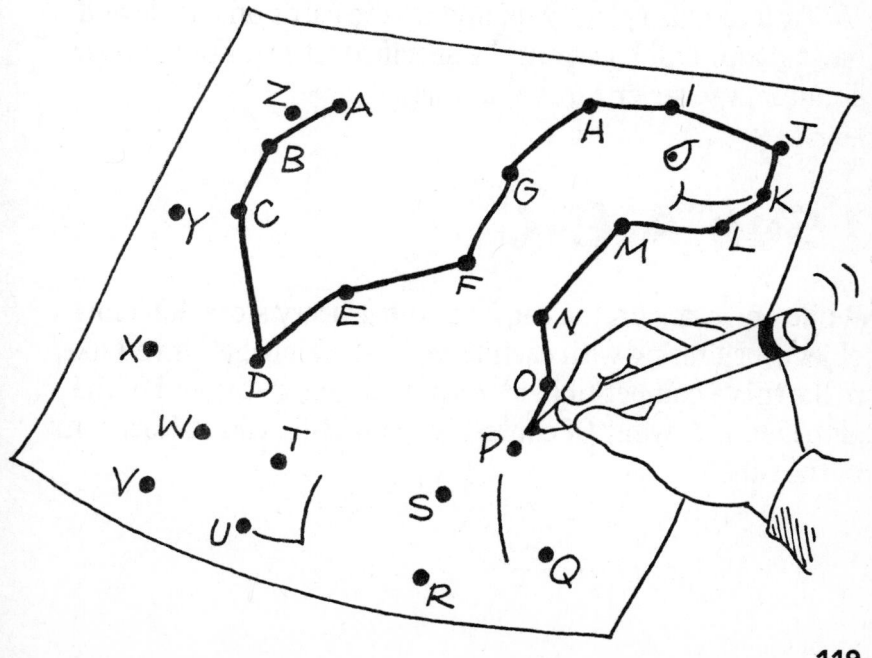

Give Me an "A"

Index cards or paper
Pen or marker
Tape

Print the letters of the alphabet on index cards and tape
several cards onto windows, walls, furniture, and other items
around the house. Tell your child what each letter is, then
have her bring you the letter you request. Or show your child
an object, such as an apple, and have her bring you the letter
"A." You can also play by mixing up the cards on a table and
having your child pick out the specified letters. For younger
children, use fewer cards at a time.

I See A-B-C

While on a walk, in the car, or at the grocery store, look for
objects beginning with each letter of the alphabet. If you like,
make this a competition, and whoever gets to the end of the
alphabet first, wins. Of course, let your child win at least some
of the time!

Word Recognition

Index cards
Pen or marker
Old magazines
Photographs (optional)
Scissors
Glue

Once your child can recognize the letters of the alphabet, you may want to start practicing simple word recognition. On one set of index cards, write some simple words, such as cat, dog, or bird. On another set, draw or cut out magazine pictures that illustrate the words you have chosen. Lay all the cards on the table, face up, and have your child match each word to the corresponding picture. Try name recognition by using photographs of your child, siblings, friends, relatives, and so on. Write the name of each person on an index card and have your child match the photo to the appropriate name.

Raisin Play

Toothpicks
Raisins
Paper
Pen, crayon, or marker

Put a raisin at the tip of each toothpick; the raisins will
connect the toothpicks and keep them from being easily
jostled apart. On a piece of paper, draw letters and shapes that
correspond in size to the toothpicks. Have your child connect
the toothpicks to create each letter or shape. You may not
need to draw the letters or shapes for older children. Keep in
mind that your child will eat some of the raisins (which makes
the activity more fun), so keep plenty on hand.

My Name

Paper
Pen or marker
Clear contact paper
Crayon or marker
Damp cloth

Help your child learn to print her name. Draw two parallel solid lines with a broken line in the middle. Print your child's first and last name on the lines, and cover the sheet with clear contact paper. Your child can use a crayon or marker to trace over her name and wipe it off with a damp cloth when finished.

Name Game

Index cards
Pen or marker

Print each letter in your child's name on an index card. Lay them out to spell your child's name. Mix them up and have her try to put them back in the proper order.

X's and O's

Paper
Pen, marker, or crayons

Print one letter at the top and center of a sheet of paper. Below this, write many letters of the alphabet in no particular pattern, spreading them over the sheet of paper. Have your child circle the letters that match the one printed at the top. Have her place an "X" over the ones that do not match. For a variation, use pictures cut from old magazines and have your child identify the pictures that begin with the letter you have written.

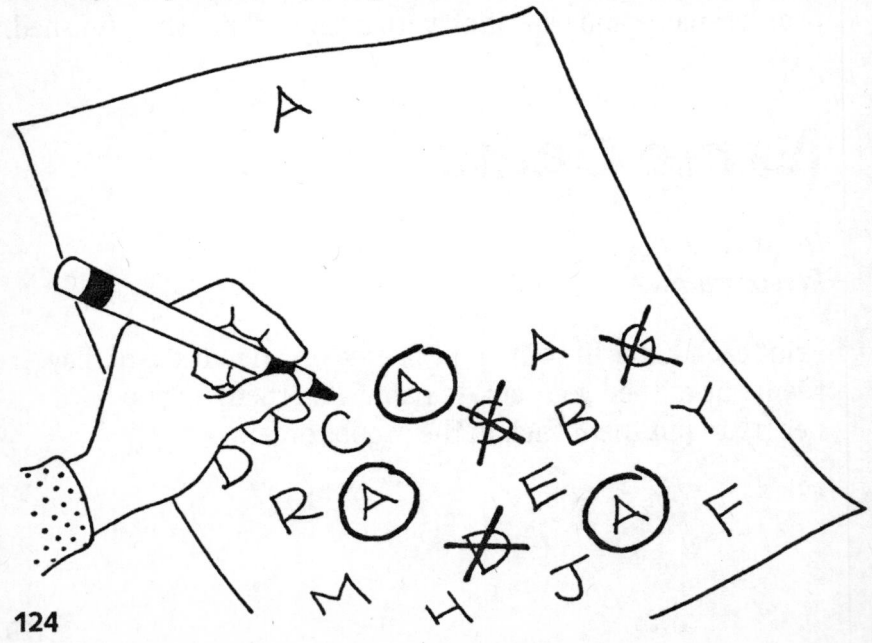

MATHEMATICS

When you think about math, you probably think "arithmetic"—the adding, subtracting, multiplying, and dividing you did when you first started school. The truth is that mathematics, the subject that incorporates numbers, shapes, patterns, estimation, and measurement, is much broader than that. Although we may not always realize it, math is everywhere, all around us, present in our world all the time—in the workplace, in our homes, and in life in general. Math is a very important skill, one we all need in our technological world, as well as in our everyday lives. Encourage your children to think of themselves as mathematicians who can reason and solve problems.

The good news is that most children enter school with the skills they need to succeed in math. They are curious about quantities, patterns, and shapes. In many respects, they are natural problem solvers. You can help build your child's math confidence without being an expert yourself. You can instill an interest in math in your child by doing math together—by asking questions that evoke thinking in terms of numbers and amounts and playing games that deal with such things as logic, reason, estimation, direction, classification, and time.

Teach your child that math is a part of the real world. Shopping, traveling, gardening, meal planning, cooking, eating, even laundry are all opportunities that allow you to apply math to your daily routine. Many activities throughout this book deal with cooking, sorting, patterns, and so on. Use them, as well as the following activities, as a fun way to help your child develop her math skills.

For additional information on children and math, I recommend *Family Math,* an excellent book packed with fun math activities for the whole family. The U.S. Department of Education also puts out a little book called *Helping Your Child Learn Math.* See Appendix E for more information on these and other helpful resources.

Counting

Give your child household counting assignments. Have her count all the doorknobs in the house, or all the cans in the kitchen cupboard, or all the knives, forks, and spoons in the silverware drawer. You can adapt this game for outside by counting cars as you go for a walk, birds that fly by as you play on the swings, and so on.

One, Two, Buckle My Shoe

This rhyme will help your child's counting skills. Try showing her objects in groups of one, two, three, and so on, as you recite the rhyme together.

One, two, buckle my shoe;
Three, four, close the door;
Five, six, pick up sticks;
Seven, eight, lay them straight;
Nine, ten, a big fat hen.

Number Fun

Index cards or small pieces of paper
Pen or marker
Tape

Write the numbers 1 to 10 on index cards or separate sheets of paper. Tape them on the windows around your house and ask your child to bring you a particular number. When she has mastered this, have her count objects, such as the number of plates on the table, and bring you the card with the correct number.

Food Count

Empty egg carton
Pen or marker
Small food items (raisins, cereal, chocolate chips, candies)

Write the numbers 1 to 12 on the individual sections of an egg carton. Have your child count out each number using small food items. Then have her fill the numbered section with the correct number of items. Once the sections are filled, work in reverse, having your child identify each number, count the pieces, then eat them!

Number Match-Up

Index cards
Pen or marker
Old magazines (optional)
Scissors (optional)
Glue (optional)

Make up two sets of index cards. On one set write numbers from 1 to 10, or higher. On the other set, draw (or cut out from magazines) pictures of objects that correspond to the numbers of the first set. Lay all the cards on the table, face up, and have your child match each numbered card to the card with the corresponding number of objects.

I Spy

This word game can help develop your child's shape and color recognition skills. As you drive or walk along, say "I spy with my little eye something that is orange," or "... something that is square." Your child will have fun guessing what it is you see. Take turns guessing what the other sees.

Calendar Math

Calendar
Markers or stickers (optional)

Read the calendar with your child every day. Include the
weekday name, the month name, the date of the month, and
the year. For example, you may say, "Today is Tuesday. That
means yesterday was _____ (Monday), and tomorrow will be
_____(Wednesday)," or "Today is the 10th of March. That
means yesterday was the ____(9th), and tomorrow will be the
____(11th)." If possible, allow your child to place a sticker on,
or mark off, each day as it is read.

Thirty Days Has September

Teach your child this rhyme about the number of days in each
month:

Thirty days has September,
April, June, and November.
All the rest have thirty-one,
Save February, which alone,
Has twenty-eight and one day more,
We add to it one year in four.

Telling Time

In these days of digital everything, your child may not see many conventional clocks, but telling time the "old way" is still a skill she should learn.

Colored construction paper
Scissors
Paper plate
Paper fastener
Crayon, pen, or marker

Make a play clock for your child to practice telling time. Cut big and little hands out of colored construction paper and attach them to a paper plate with a paper fastener. Using a crayon, pen, or marker, number the clock appropriately. Your child can move the hands around the clock as she learns the basics of telling time. (Most young children will not learn all the details of telling time—to the quarter hour, to the minute, and so on—but, if they know their numbers up to twelve, they can certainly learn to tell time on the hour and maybe even on the half hour.)

Glitter Shapes

Construction paper
Glue
Glitter or Colorful Creative Salt (see Appendix A)

On construction paper, use glue to draw various shapes:
square, rectangle, triangle, heart, circle, oval, star. Have your
child sprinkle glitter (or Colorful Creative Salt) over the
shapes. Shake off the extra glitter and practice the names of
each shape.

Shape Match-Up

Colored construction paper
White construction paper
Pen or marker
Scissors

Cut basic shapes (circle, square, rectangle, triangle, heart, and
so on) out of colored construction paper. Trace all the shapes
onto a piece of white construction paper. Have your child
match the colored shapes to those drawn on the white paper.

What's Different?

Various household objects

Give your child a group of objects, maybe three or four, that are related in some way: eating utensils, drawing tools, books, fruit, and so on. Add one item that doesn't fit with the rest of the objects. Have your child identify the object that doesn't belong and tell you why.

Cards

Deck of playing cards

Pull one red card and one black card out of a deck of playing cards, and place them on the table or floor. Give your child a small stack of cards and have her practice sorting them into either the red pile or the black pile. You can also do this with each of the four suits or with the numbers on the cards.

GEOGRAPHY

Geography is the study of the earth, divided into five major themes: location (where it is); place (what makes a place special, both physically and culturally); interaction (between people and the environment); movement (of people, products, and information); and regions (areas defined by distinctive characteristics). Geography is a way of thinking, asking questions, observing, and appreciating the world around us.

You can help your child develop an interest in geography by providing interesting activities for her, and by prompting her to ask questions about her surroundings. To help you think geographically, and to help your child build precise mental images, try to use basic geographical terms whenever possible, i.e., west or north, climate, highway, river, and desert. Expose your child to lots of maps and let her see you use maps regularly.

The following activities are only a few examples of the many ways children learn geography. They are informal and easy to do, and are designed to help you find ways to include geographic thinking in your child's early experiences.

Play City

Markers
Large sheet of paper

Using markers on a large sheet of paper, draw an imaginary
city big enough for your child's cars and trucks. Be sure to
include some landmarks familiar to your child: bank, grocery
store, gas station, park, hospital, school, post office, train
tracks, and so on. Tape the finished city to the floor so your
child can travel around the city with her cars, trucks, dolls,
and fire engines. For a more permanent city, use paints on
strong cardboard or wood. Glue milk cartons or small boxes
onto the map to make buildings. For a variation, make an
imaginary airport or farm.

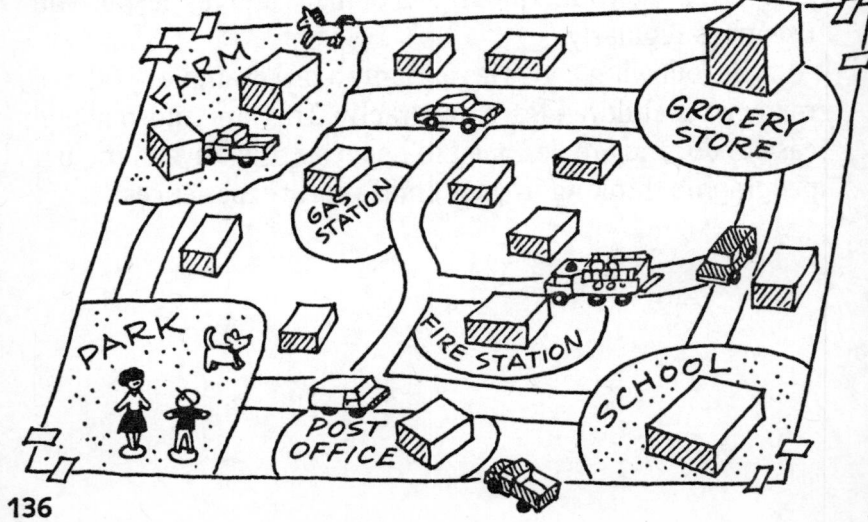

Treasure Hunt

Paper
Pens or markers
Small toys or other treats

Have a treasure hunt in the park, on the beach, in your
backyard, or in your house. Draw a map that leads to the
treasure, which can be several small toys, cars, or other items.

North, South, East, West

Small toy, book, or household object

Show your child north, south, east, and west by using your
home as a reference point. If your child's bedroom faces east,
point out the sun rising in the morning. Show the sunset
through a window facing west. Once your child has her
directional bearings, hide a small toy or household object
somewhere in the house. Give directions to its location: two
steps to the north, three steps west, and so on.

Where Do We Live?

Map of your city, town, or neighborhood

Look for your city, town, or neighborhood on a map. Point out
your home's location and the location of relatives' and best
friends' homes. Find the school your child will attend and
show your child its location in relation to your house and
street. Find the nearest park, lake, mountain, or other cultural
or physical feature on the map and talk about how these
features affect your life. Living near the ocean may make your
climate moderate, prairies may provide an open path for high
winds, and mountains may block some weather fronts.

Draw a Map

Paper
Pens or markers

Help your child draw a simple map of her neighborhood.
Include familiar and personal landmarks on her map: the
mailbox, the store, the playground, her friend's house, the fire
station. Take this map with you on your walks and point out
the landmarks as you go. On your walk, collect natural
materials, such as acorns and leaves, to use for an art project.
At home, map the location where you found these items. You
can also draw maps of your yard, your house, or your child's
bedroom.

My Neighborhood

Take a walk around your neighborhood and look at what makes it unique. Point out differences from and similarities to other places. Can your child distinguish various types of homes and shops? Look at the buildings and talk about their uses. Are there features built to conform with the weather or topography? Do the shapes of some buildings indicate how they were used in the past or how they are used now? These observations help children understand the character of a place.

Litter Patrol

Disposing of waste is a problem of geographic dimensions.

Bag for litter
Gloves
Stick with pointed end

Go on a neighborhood litter patrol with your child. You may want to wear gloves and use a stick with a pointed end to pick up the litter. Talk about litter, garbage, and recycling and how we can help control and take care of our surroundings.

Language Play

Learn simple words in different languages. Teach your child to count to ten in other languages and to say simple words like "hello," "good-bye," and "thank you." Have a theme day when you locate a country on the map and talk about the unique aspects of its location. Talk about the language spoken there and, if possible, learn several words in that language. Serve a special lunch or snack that originated, or is popular, in that country.

People, Places, and Things

Maps

Go around your house and find the origins of various objects. Look at the labels of the clothes you wear and think of where your food was grown. Why do bananas come from Central America? Why does the milk come from the local dairy? Maybe your climate is too cold for bananas, and the milk is too perishable to travel far. Talk about where your ancestors came from, and use a map to find the countries. Use a map to show your child where family and friends live now.

Coin and Stamp Collecting

Coins and/or stamps from your own and other countries
Small box, notebook, or coin and stamp collecting books
Glue and tape

Start your preschooler on a coin and/or stamp collection. Ask friends and family traveling abroad to collect coins for you. Compare the coins and see what information they contain about the country. Stamps tell many different things about a country—from its political leadership to its native bird life. Show your child how to remove stamps from your incoming mail by soaking them in a small amount of warm water. Give her special notebooks into which she can glue the stamps and tape the coins, or save them in a small box.

Cloud Watching

Climate is an important part of a region's geographic character. On a warm and lazy afternoon, lay down in the grass with your child and watch the clouds drift across the sky. Talk about how clouds are formed (water evaporates from the earth and condenses into small droplets) and what happens when clouds touch the earth (fog). Help her pick out shapes in the clouds and, afterward, have her draw what she saw.

BASIC BOTANY

Your child's early efforts at gardening may be clumsy, but she will learn the basics of botany by getting dirty and having fun. You can teach your child how seeds develop into four basic parts—the roots, the stems, the leaves, and the flower that, in turn, produces new seed. She will learn that plants eat minerals through their roots and that earthworms fertilize the soil and aerate it so that roots can breathe better. Teach your child how the leaves inhale carbon dioxide and exhale oxygen, which is why nature needs a balance between animals and plants. Explain that plants are the only living things that make their own food, chlorophyll.

Use the following activities to teach your child, in an informal and fun way, the basic principles of botany.

Growing Plants

Seeds
Shallow dish of water
Planters
Potting soil

Your preschooler will be fascinated to see how plants grow
from seeds or cuttings. Soak seeds from an orange, apple,
grapefruit, lemon, or lime in water for a day or two. Fill
several planters with potting soil and place three or four seeds
in each one about half an inch deep. Water the seeds, place the
pots in a sunny spot, and watch for the green shoots to grow.
You can try plantings seeds in a pattern or shape: a letter,
number, square, or circle.

Garlic Clove

Garlic clove
Potting soil
Small pot

Plant an unpeeled garlic clove in potting soil, pointed end up.
Cover completely, water every few days, and keep in the sun.

Carrots and Beets

Carrots or beets
Shallow dish of water
Small pot
Potting soil

Cut two inches off the top of a carrot or beet. Set cut side down in a dish with half an inch of water. Change the water every one or two days. When roots appear plant your carrot or beet, cut side down, in a pot of moist soil. Set it in a sunny window and keep it wet.

Sweet Potato Vine

Sweet potato
Toothpicks
Glass of water
String

Stick three toothpicks in the sides of an old sweet potato. Set it in a glass of water with the toothpicks resting on the rim of the glass. The water should just cover the tip of the sweet potato. Put the glass in a place where the vine will get filtered sunlight. Pin up some strings so the plant can climb.

Avocado Tree

Avocado seed
5-inch pot
Potting soil

Dry an avocado seed for a couple of days, then peel the papery brown skin off. Plant, base down, about two-thirds down in a pot of soil, leaving the pointed tip exposed until the seed germinates (thirty to ninety days). You can keep the pot in the sun, or well-watered in a dark cupboard for a stronger root system. When the seed sprouts, leave one new shoot at the top and pinch off the rest of the new growth. This will allow all the plant's energy to go into the one remaining shoot, which should then grow into a lush, bushy tree.

Lima Bean Sprouts

Lima beans
Shallow dish
Water

Put lima beans in a dish and fill with water. Place the dish in a sunny window and watch how the beans change daily.

Flower Tinting

This is a good activity to show your child how plants drink water through their stalks and where the water goes.

Clear glass or vase
Water
Food coloring
White carnation or daisy

Fill a clear glass or vase halfway with water and add enough food coloring to tint the water a bright color. Add a white carnation or daisy and watch the flower change color over the next few hours. You can also do this experiment with celery. In fact, this may be great way to encourage a reluctant eater. After all, purple celery is bound to taste better than the green variety!

CHAPTER 7
Music, Dance, and Drama

"The events of childhood do not pass, but repeat themselves like seasons of the year."
—*Eleanor Farjeon*

Music, dance, and drama are an essential part of our children's general education. Through the study of music, dance, and drama, children acquire knowledge, skills, and attitudes that influence them throughout their lives. In addition to learning music for its own sake, children learn coordination, goal-setting, concentration, and cooperation. Dance activities also offer many benefits for children, encouraging mental and emotional development while enhancing motor skills. Drama involves mind, body, and imagination, and is essential to a child's full development.

This chapter provides simple ideas that will help you stimulate your child's development in these three areas. The following activities will cultivate your child's sense of rhythm, allow your child to experience movement as it relates to music and rhythm, and encourage your child in creative play.

MUSIC AND RHYTHM

As a parent, you can encourage your child's love of music and nurture his musical talents in a number of ways: listen to music programs and recordings together, attend musical events, make music as a family, and praise children for their musical activities and accomplishments. As a result of music-listening and music-making experiences, children can become better listeners and develop musical intelligence.

Listening to music, moving to music, and playing musical games are the best musical activities for small children. The following ideas will help you begin to develop your child's sense of music and rhythm.

Tambourine

Corn kernels, dried beans, small pasta, cereal, and so on
2 paper plates
Glue or staples
Hole punch
Ribbon
Crayons, markers, stickers for decoration

Place corns, beans, pasta, or cereal onto a paper plate, cover with the second plate, and glue or staple the rims of the plates together. When the glue is dry, punch holes around the rims and lace ribbon through the holes. Let your child decorate with crayons, markers, stickers, and so on.

Rhythm Blocks

2 4-inch pieces of a two-by-four piece of wood

Give your child two pieces of wood to use as rhythm blocks; make sure that the blocks are smooth and the edges are not too sharp. Your child can bang the blocks together in time to a rhythmic beat.

Pie Plate Tambourine

Aluminum pie plate
Hammer and nail
6 to 8 flattened bottle caps
String

Using a hammer and nail, an adult should make six to eight holes around the edge of an aluminum pie plate, and one hole in the center of the same number of flattened bottle caps. Let your child pull a piece of string through each bottle cap and thread it through a hole in the pie plate. Tie a knot tight enough to hold the bottle cap in place, but allow enough slack so that the cap can move freely and hit the pie plate when shaken. Attach each cap in this way; shake to play.

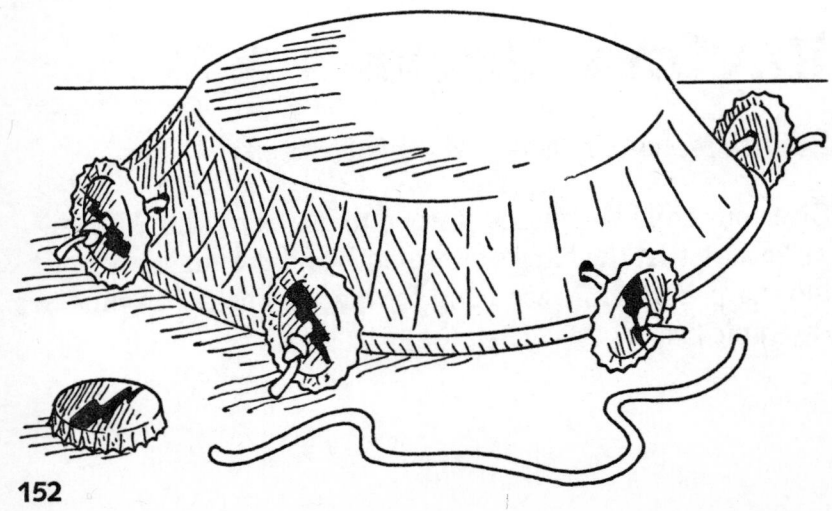

Shakers

*Plastic medicine bottles in various sizes, soap bottles, small
pop-top juice cans, or small aluminum pie or tart pans
Popcorn, rice, dried beans, pennies, and other noise-making
items
Glue gun or tape*

Collect an assortment of variously sized plastic medicine
bottles, soap bottles, small juice cans, or small aluminum pie
or tart pans. Partially fill each container with anything that
creates noise: popcorn, rice, dried beans, pennies, and so on.
Use a variety of items, as each makes a different sound. If the
container has a lid, or if using aluminum pie pans, secure
them with glue from a hot glue gun. If the container doesn't
have a lid, tape it shut.

Sandpaper Blocks

2 4-inch pieces of a two-by-four piece of wood
Sandpaper
Glue

Glue sandpaper onto the wood, and rub together for an interesting sound.

Noise Blower

Empty cardboard tube (toilet paper or paper towel rolls)
Wax paper
Elastic band
Crayons, markers, ribbon, stickers, fabric, construction paper,
*   and other items for decoration*

Cover one end of a cardboard tube with a piece of wax paper, using an elastic band to hold the wax paper in place. Blow and hum into the uncovered end to make a vibrating sound. Older children can make this for themselves, decorating the tube with crayons, markers, stickers, scraps of ribbon, fabric, or construction paper.

Milk Carton Guitar

Cardboard milk carton (half-gallon size)
Sharp knife
Tape
Yardstick
Saw
45-inch length of nylon fishing line

Make a guitar that your child can really play! Tape shut the top of a clean, empty half-gallon milk carton. With a sharp knife, cut vertical slits, big enough to slip a yardstick through, in two sides of the carton, two-thirds up from the bottom. Cut a notch about a half inch deep near each end of the yardstick with a saw and insert through the carton. Position the carton near the center of the yardstick. Make a loop in one end of the length of fishing line and slip it over the notch on the top of the yardstick. Pull the line over the top of the carton and loop it around the notch at the other end of the yardstick. Tie securely and pull the carton to one end of the yardstick. To play the guitar, strum the string near the top edge of the milk carton with one hand. Pinch the string to the yardstick with the other hand to change pitches.

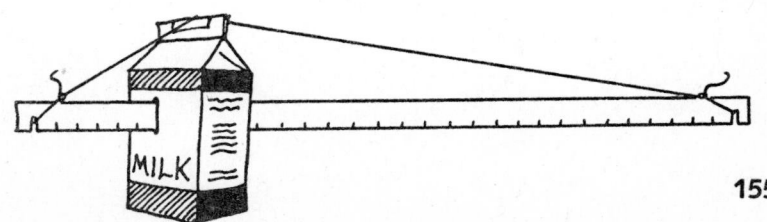

MOVEMENT AND DANCE

For young children, dance offers an avenue for exploration, discovery, and the development of natural instincts for movement. Dance has many physical benefits—among them, increased flexibility, improved circulation, development of muscle tone and strength, and improved posture, balance, and coordination. But, although dance can be great exercise and an artistic expression of mind and body, for young children, dance is usually just plain fun. It's also a great way to help children "shake their sillies out"!

Let's Pretend

Have your child tell a story by acting it out with body movements, or ask him to move with different types of walks (down-
hill, on parade, stiff, up stairs) or pretend to use different
kinds of vehicles (bicycle, skateboard, car, horse, and so on).
This will provide your child with the opportunity to explore
and invent movement.

Music and Movement

*Homemade rhythm instruments, real musical instruments,
  such as piano or guitar, or recorded music*

The goal of this activity is to have your child experience
movement as it relates to music or rhythm. Play different
types of music and have your child physically express how the
music makes him feel: run for fast music, tiptoe for soft
music, hop and bounce for happy music, march for a parade
tune, and so on. You can also tap out a rhythmic beat and
encourage your child to clap or hop in time to the beat.

Exercise Class

Pretend to have an exercise class in your living room. You can dress in exercise wear if you like, and take turns being the "instructor." Include both locomotor movements (walking, running, jumping, skipping, and so on) and nonlocomotor movements (bending, stretching, twisting, swinging, and so on). Vary the size, level, and direction of these basics to allow your child to discover a large number of movements that can be combined to form basic dance steps. You can also make a point to include these movements in other games you play, such as Simon Says (page 54) or Follow the Leader (page 49).

Moving Questions

Ask your child questions like, "How many ways can you balance yourself besides standing?" and "How many different ways can you move your head (arms, leg, upper body)?" Such questions will help your child become aware of his body and its relationship to other people and the environment.

Circle Dances

Circle dances are a great way to stress body movement. Whether you dance with several children or just one, circle dances can be a lot of fun. Try old favorites like Hokey Pokey, Looby Loo, Ring around the Rosie, Mulberry Bush, Skip to My Lou, or London Bridge. For more ideas, your local library will likely have song books, cassettes, or videos by many popular children's performers.

DRAMATIC PLAY

Children of all ages love to pretend. As toddlers, they first enter the world of make-believe by engaging in activities they see around them and by putting themselves in the place of others. This activity involves mind, body, and imagination. It is a child's rehearsal for life and is essential to a child's full development.

As children grow older, their play develops more structure. They act out favorite stories, create original situations from life experiences, and imagine themselves in fantasy worlds where anything is possible. If they are encouraged in this kind of play at home, they become ready for creative drama by the time they enter school.

The following activities will encourage your child's dramatic play.

Post Office

Unopened "junk mail"
Unused return envelopes from your mail
Stickers from magazine and record clubs
Inexpensive stationery
One-cent stamps (optional)
Date stamp or other rubber stamp and ink pad
Bank slips

Help your child open a post office of his own. Save unopened junk mail, unused return envelopes from mail you receive, and stickers from magazine and record clubs. You may want to provide him with inexpensive stationery and authentic one-cent stamps. Give him a date stamp or other rubber stamp and ink pad, and bank slips for official looking forms.

Tickle Trunk

Empty trunk or large box
Adult clothes and props

You can encourage your child's dramatic play by setting up a
Tickle Trunk full of props for him. Fill a trunk or box with
adult clothes, shoes, hats, scarves, gloves, and costume jewelry
to use for dress-up. Old suits are great, as are Hawaiian shirts,
vests, baseball hats, wigs, boots, and slippers (for girls, include
old bridesmaid dresses, costume jewelry, nightgowns, and
purses). Great items can be found at garage sales or local
thrift shops. A Tickle Trunk will be an invaluable part of your
child's dramatic play and items can be added for years.

Hospital

Stuffed animals
Pillows
Blankets
White clothes for uniforms
Thermometer
Bandages
Medicine measuring spoon
Sling (cloth diaper or other material folded into a triangle)

Using friends, stuffed animals, or cooperative parents for patients, help your child set up a hospital or doctor's office. Lay pillows and blankets in a corner of the room. Give the "nurse" or "doctor" white clothing for his uniform. Show him how to take temperatures with a thermometer, bandage arms and legs, and give medicine. Make a sling from a flat cloth diaper or other piece of material folded into a triangle. Take turns playing the doctor, nurse, patient, and visitor.

Barber Shop

Brushes
Combs
Empty hair spray bottle filled with water
Shaving cream
Popsicle stick or old credit card
Towel

Help your child set up a barber shop. Give him brushes, combs, an empty hair spray bottle filled with water, and shaving cream. A wooden Popsicle stick or an old credit card can be used as a razor. Use a towel to wipe off shaving cream and water. Take turns being the barber.

Restaurant

Tablecloth or other linens
Vase with flowers or other centerpiece
Candle (optional)
Menu

Use table linens, flowers (real or other) in a vase, and a candle. Take the customer's coat, show him to his seat, give him a menu, and let him order lunch or dinner. Take turns being the waiter and the customer.

Beauty Salon

Brushes
Curlers
Hair bows
Empty hair spray bottle filled with water
Towel
Nail polish (optional)

Give your child brushes, curlers, hair bows, and an empty hair spray bottle filled with water to use in his beauty salon. Use friends, siblings, or parents for clients, and take turns being the hairdresser. Use a towel to absorb water used during play. For girls, apply nail polish on fingers and toes as a special treat.

Grocery Store

Empty food boxes, plastic containers, nonbreakable jars
Old purse or wallet
Play money
Scissors
Store coupons
Grocery list
Paper grocery bag

Help your child set up a grocery store by saving empty boxes, plastic containers, nonbreakable jars, and so on. Give him an old purse or wallet containing play money and coins. He can practice his scissor skills by cutting out unwanted coupons to use in his store. Help him make a shopping list and give him a paper bag for his groceries.

Bakery

Aprons
White paper lunch bag
Rolling pin
Cookie cutters
Playdough
Prepared cookie dough (optional)
Plastic knife (optional)
Cookie sheet (optional)

Give your child an apron and a white paper lunch bag to wear as a baker's hat. Have him use a rolling pin and cookie cutters to "bake" cookies, pies, and cakes out of playdough. Or use a roll of prepared cookie dough: Give your child a plastic knife, have him slice off cookies, and place them on a cookie sheet for real baking.

167

Dentist

Cup with water
Bowl for spitting
Paper napkin
Flashlight
Toothbrush
Small toys for "prizes"

Because water is involved, this game is best played in the
kitchen or bathroom. Take turns being the dentist and patient.
The dentist tucks a paper napkin into the patient's collar to
protect his shirt, then uses the flashlight to look into his
mouth. The dentist may want to brush the patient's teeth,
then advise him to rinse his mouth and spit into the bowl. As
the patient leaves, the dentist can offer him a "prize."

CHAPTER 8
Arts and Crafts

"The parents exist to teach the child, but they must also learn what the child has to teach them; and the child has a very great deal to teach them."
—*Arnold Bennett*

Arts and crafts projects provide great opportunities for creative play for your child. Through her work with arts and crafts, your child will learn to think creatively and develop skills in drawing, painting, sculpting, designing, and crafting. Well-chosen arts and crafts projects will help your child develop concentration and coordination, as well as organizational and manipulative skills. They will promote a sense of great achievement, and are fun and exciting for children of all ages.

That said, one of the main problems I've always had with arts and crafts projects is what to do with all the wonderful things your child so busily and happily creates? Children can produce an enormous volume of work in a short amount of time. Multiply that by two or three children, and you can have a major problem on your hands! Here are some ideas that might help:

- Always be on the alert for creative ways to use your child's art, i.e., as gifts or gift wrap (see Appendix C).
- Display your child's art around the house, not just on the refrigerator. Visit an art framing shop and ask them to save their mat scraps for you. You may get some pieces that are great for either mounting or framing your child's work.
- Make Grandma or other relatives a calendar of your child's art. Save your little artist's work throughout the year. As the new year approaches, visit local businesses and collect free calendars. Glue your child's art onto the picture part of each month, so a new masterpiece will be displayed each time the calendar changes.
- Create a "portfolio" for your child. Using a three-ring binder and plastic page protectors, save some of your child's outstanding creations. Be sure to date or write your child's age on each work of art. For extra-large or 3-D projects, take a photo or two and put those in the binder. (The project itself will have to go eventually!)

When the day comes (and it will) to get rid of some of the pictures and projects your child has created, be sure to do it in a sensitive way. Chances are she will not miss the picture that was hanging on the refrigerator for a month, but finding it crumpled up in the kitchen waste basket is sure to make her feel that you don't really value her work. Take items directly to the outdoor trash containers just before the garbage is picked up to save you and your child some heartache.

Old phone books come in very handy for children's little projects. When your child is coloring, painting, or gluing, open the phone book and place your child's paper on a clean page. Then simply turn the page for a clean working surface for the next project. This way, you won't have to worry about finding scrap paper to line your child's workspace, and you won't have to clean paint and glue off your kitchen table nearly as often.

Here are some activities you can use to introduce your child to the world of art. Remember that your attitudes make strong impressions on your child; encourage her to experiment. Arts and crafts projects are a form of self-expression, and your child should know that there is no right or wrong way to create art.

DRAWING

Drawing is probably the first art form your child will experience. It allows your child to express herself creatively and helps the development of her small muscles and hand/eye coordination. Drawing is simple and it can be done anywhere and at anytime. It is something most of us do, in some form or another, all our lives.

Give your child a little variety in her drawing tools and materials. Try using pens, pencil crayons, chalk, and markers. For drawing paper, use construction paper, newspaper, fine sandpaper, or cut-open grocery bags in varying sizes. Your child will also enjoy drawing and tracing shapes, such as circles, triangles, and stars cut from different types of paper.

Stained-Glass Crayons

Warning: These come out looking a little like peanut butter cups. Your child just may decide to take a bite!

Broken crayon pieces
Muffin tin, greased
Aluminum foil (optional)

This is a good project to use up all those broken crayon pieces. Remove any paper from the crayons and place the pieces in a well-greased muffin tin (or line the tin with aluminum foil). Place the tin in a 400-degree oven for a few minutes, until the crayons melt. Remove from the oven and cool completely before removing from the tin. If you mixed crayon colors in the tins, the circles will have a stained glass effect and are great for coloring.

Rainbow Crayons

Beautiful, and easy for little hands to hold!

Broken crayon pieces
Clean, empty tin cans
Pot of hot water
Empty, plastic 35-mm film canisters

This is another good way to use broken crayons. Remove any paper from the crayons and sort them by color. Place the pieces, one color at a time, in the empty tin cans. Set the tin cans in a pot of very hot or boiling water until the crayons melt. Pour a small amount (approximately a quarter inch) into each film canister. When the wax hardens, add a second color in the same way. When you are done, you will have a crayon rainbow of layered colors.

Clothespin Crayons

Clothespins
Crayons
Paper

Clip a clothespin around a crayon and encourage your child to draw while holding onto the clothespin instead of the crayon. The idea is to try to do the same old things in new and different ways. Clipping a clothespin onto a crayon will make coloring seem different and interesting, if only for a few minutes.

Rainbow Drawing

Crayons
Tape
Paper

Tape two or more crayons together and have your child draw a picture. You will get some interesting effects with this double and triple layering of color. If you want to use true rainbow colors, you will need violet, indigo, blue, green, yellow, orange, and red.

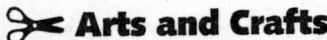

Thumbprint Mice

Stamp pad
Paper
Crayons or markers

Have your child press her thumb on a stamp pad and then press it onto paper. Show your child how to draw a mouse tail and ears on the thumbprint to complete each mouse. Do this several times to make a mouse family. Use your own thumb and perhaps one of an older or younger sibling, then compare the different sizes each makes.

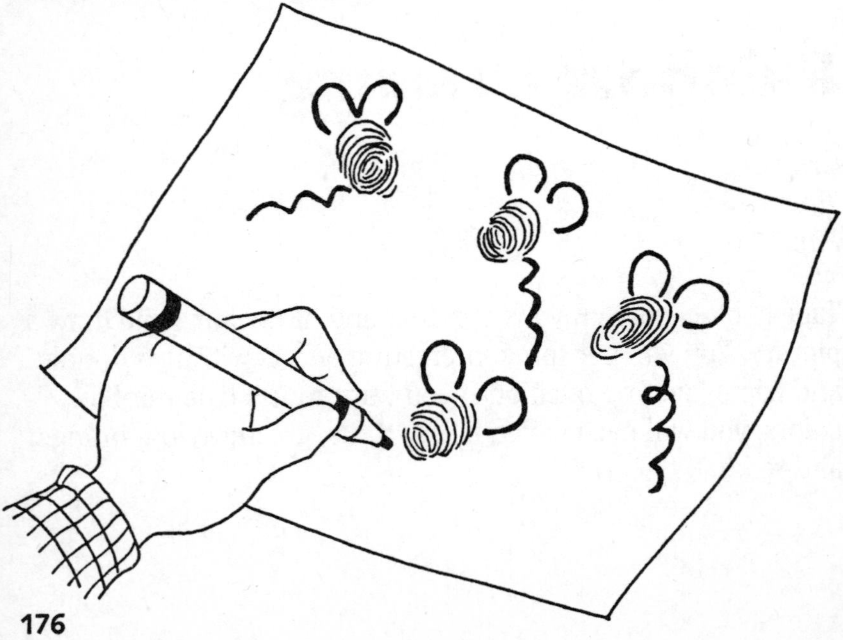

Self-Portraits

Very large sheet of newsprint or other paper
Markers, crayons, or paint

Have your child lie down on the floor on the paper. Trace around her, then let her fill in the details with markers, crayons, or paint. Tell her to be as detailed as possible: What is her hair like? What color are her eyes? What clothes is she wearing? When finished, hang her portrait in her room or on her door where she can admire it.

Nature Colors

Plants and flowers collected on a walk
Crayons
Paper

Go on a walk with your child, and bring home a variety of plants and flowers, such as grass, leaves, dandelions, and so on. Spread them out on a table in your backyard and encourage your child to draw a picture using only crayons in colors that match the items you have collected.

Fruit Rub

Cardboard
Scissors
Paper
Paper clips
Crayons

Cut a fruit shape, such as an apple, orange, or banana, out of cardboard. Place the cardboard shape between two sheets of paper and clip them together with a paper clip. Give your child an appropriately colored crayon, and have her rub over the paper lightly, to make a red apple or yellow banana appear.

Crayon Rubbings

Paper or cut-open grocery bags
Small textured objects
Crayons

Place paper or cut-open grocery bags over textured objects, such as leaves, string, doilies, paper clips, fabric, tiles, coins, cardboard shapes, or bricks. Have your child rub a crayon on the paper. Shift the paper and use different colors for interesting patterns.

Wet Chalk Drawings

6 tablespoons sugar
¼ cup water
Colored chalk
Paper, white

Mix together sugar and water and pour over the chalk; let soak for ten minutes. Have your child use the wet chalk to draw on white paper. If you use white chalk, draw on colored paper.

Picture a Story

Paper
Crayons or markers

Have your child draw a series of four or five pictures. Have her then dictate a story to go with each picture. You can write the story on the bottom of the picture as it is told.

Hand Drawings

Paper
Crayons or markers
Nail polish (optional)
Sparkles or small beads
Glue

Place your child's hands on a piece of paper and trace around them. Give your child crayons, markers, or nail polish and have her paint the nails of her drawing. Use glue and sparkles or small beads to add rings, watches, and other details. For variety, try tracing your child's feet, then have her trace your feet and compare sizes. Color the feet and add nail polish and funny rings with crayons or markers.

Scribble Drawing

Paper
Crayons

Show your child how to scribble on a piece of white paper with a crayon, using big circular motions to form loops. Then have your child color in each loop with a different color, creating a very pretty and unique design every time.

Secret Messages

White crayon or wax candle
Paper, white
Tempera paints
Paintbrush

Use a white crayon or wax candle to write a message or draw a picture on a piece of white paper. Your child can then paint over the paper with tempera paint to see the picture or message appear.

Blindfold Drawing

Blindfold
Crayons or markers
Paper

Place a blindfold on your child, then have her draw on paper with crayons or markers. When her drawing is complete, remove the blindfold and take turns looking for hidden shapes or objects in the picture.

Bark Drawing

Tree bark
Crayons, pens, or paint

Go for a walk and collect tree bark. At home, use crayons, pens, or paint to draw pictures on the bark. Talk about how people used tree bark before paper was invented, and how paper comes from trees.

PAINTING

Painting is a wonderful outlet for a child's creativity. Large pieces of paper, pots of paint in vivid colors, big paintbrushes, and a painter's smock will keep your little artist happy on many a rainy afternoon. Provide a good work space, keep supplies handy, and make cleanup part of the project. Work outdoors when you can, and let nature provide further inspiration.

The best kind of paint for young children is poster paint, also known as tempera paint, which you can buy at any art store in premixed liquid form or as a powder that must be mixed with water. You can also make your own poster paint using the recipes in Appendix A. Children rarely need more than three colors: red, blue, and yellow. Teach your child how to mix these colors to create others. Tempera blocks are also available; they are practical because they don't have to be diluted and can't be spilled, making cleanup easier. In addition, tempera blocks are economical, since they are less expensive and last a very long time; however, your child will probably not find them as fun as the slick liquid paints.

Paper can be purchased from an art supply store, but consider some of the following alternatives. Newsprint is a wonderful paper for painting; roll-ends can be purchased cheaply from a newspaper publisher. Visit your local printer and ask if you can leave an empty box for a week or two; she may agree to fill it with all kinds of wonderful paper that would otherwise be discarded. Try fine sandpaper as an alternative art paper for a wonderful effect. For fingerpainting, use the shiny side of freezer paper that can be purchased at the grocery store. It is much cheaper than special fingerpaint paper and works just as well.

String up a line in the laundry room or kitchen to hang paintings to dry. Wet artwork can be attached to the line with clothespins. When dry, be sure to display your child's paintings prominently. And think of creative uses for some of her work; many painting projects make wonderful gift wrap or greeting cards.

Starch Painting

Bowl
Liquid starch
Liquid detergent
Paper or plastic cloth
Powdered tempera paint

Mix a small amount of detergent with liquid starch in a bowl and pour the mixture onto a painting surface, such as a tabletop, paper, or plastic cloth. Sprinkle powdered tempera paint over the starch, and let your child experiment with mixing colors.

Dipping

Paper towel
Bowls of diluted food coloring or strong watercolors

Have your child fold a piece of paper towel into a fairly small packet. Have her dip each corner of the packet into a bowl of colored dye (diluted food coloring or strong watercolors). Use a different color for each corner. Unfold the paper towel and hang to dry. You can use various types of paper; the more absorbent the paper, the faster the dye will spread. Dipped rice paper makes a nice gift wrap, but it is fairly expensive.

Fingerpainting

Fingerpaints
Paper

Fingerpainting is a wonderfully messy adventure that every child should experience after about the age of two (younger, if you can stand it!). Unfortunately, it can be a frustrating experience for parents, as the amount of work required to set up and clean up never seems to merit the five minutes (or less) most children will spend at this activity! That said, be prepared for a great big mess, and make sure your child wears an art smock. Wet the paper first to allow the paint to slide better, drop a blob of paint on the paper, and let your child go to it. Commercial fingerpaints can be bought, or make your own using the recipes in Appendix A.

String Painting

Paper
Tempera paint, liquid
String or yarn

Drop some paint onto a piece of paper and let your child make a design by dragging string through the paint and around the paper. Try it again by dipping the string in the paint and dragging it across the paper. Use different types and lengths of string and yarn for varying effects.

3-D String Painting

Bowl
Tempera paint, liquid
Liquid starch
String
Paper

For this activity, mix liquid paint and liquid starch in equal parts in a bowl. Dip some string into the paint/starch solution and drop it onto a sheet of paper. When the paint dries, the starch will make the string stick to the paper.

Drippy Painting

Paper or a cut-open brown paper bag
Tempera paint, liquid
Eyedropper, spoon, or straw

On a big sheet of paper or a cut-open brown paper bag, have
your child drip liquid tempera paints using an eyedropper,
spoon, or straw. Tip the paper in different directions to make a
design. Drip another color and tip the paper again for an
interesting result.

Air Painting

Paper
Tempera paint
Eydropper, spoon, or straw
Empty squeeze bottle

Have your child drop some paint onto a piece of paper and
disperse it by squeezing air onto it with an empty squeeze
bottle. She can also do this by blowing on the paint through a
wide plastic tube or straw. If you like, add a second and third
color. You can also try different types of paper for different
effects.

Bubble Painting

Newspaper
Liquid dishwashing detergent
Shallow dish
Tempera paint
Straw
Construction paper or other paper

Cover your child's work surface with newspaper. Pour a quarter cup liquid dishwashing detergent into a shallow dish. If you use powdered tempera paint, mix a small amount of water with the paint. Add the paint mixture or liquid tempera to the dishwashing liquid until the color is intense. Place one end of a straw into the mixture, and blow until the bubbles are almost billowing over the edge of the dish. Gently place a piece of construction paper or other paper on top of the bubbles and hold it in place until several bubbles have popped. Continue this process with different colors, blowing more bubbles as needed. To make a unique greeting card, use a piece of construction paper folded in half. When dry, your child can add drawings to the picture and sign her name.

Stencil Painting

Thin cardboard
Scissors
Paper
Tape
Sponge or brush
Tempera paint, liquid

Draw a design, letter, or animal shape on thin cardboard. Cut out the inside of the shape to make the stencil, and tape the stencil onto a sheet of paper. Show your child how to dip a sponge or brush into liquid tempera paint, then fill in the inside of the stencil with color. When finished, remove the tape and lift off the stencil to see the design.

Spray Painting

Newspaper
Paper or a cut-open brown paper bag
Tempera paint, liquid
Plant sprayer

For this activity you will want to prepare your work area well. Lay down lots of newspaper, and be prepared to offer close supervision. Place some paper or cut-open brown paper bags on the newspaper. Pour some thin paint into a plant sprayer and let your child spray it onto the paper. Use several different colors, and when the paper is dry, you will have some great gift wrap.

Balloon Painting

Balloons of various sizes
Tempera paint, liquid
Paper

Blow up balloons of various sizes and tie the ends. Hold onto the tied end, dip the balloon into liquid tempera paint, and blot it onto a sheet of paper. The resulting artwork can be displayed on the wall or used as unique gift wrap.

Foot Painting

Newspaper
Butcher or fingerpaint paper
Tempera paint or fingerpaint, liquid
Warm, soapy water in a bucket
Towel
Rubber boots or tennis shoes (optional)

Cover your floor with newspaper, then spread large sheets of butcher or fingerpaint paper on the newspapers, glossy side up. Pour about a quarter cup liquid tempera paint or fingerpaint onto the paper. Encourage your barefooted child to walk, stamp, and slide her feet through the paint to make different effects. Have a bucket of warm, soapy water and a towel ready for cleanup. For a variation, have your child wear rubber boots or tennis shoes.

Marble Painting

Marbles
Tempera paint, liquid
Paper
Flat box

Place a piece of paper into a flat box (like the box from a 24-pack of soda). Have your child drop marbles into various colors of tempera paint, then drop them into the box and roll them across the paper. Or drop some paint onto the paper and have your child roll the marbles across the paint.

Eyedropper Painting

Eyedropper
Tempera paint, liquid
Paper

Show your child how to use an eyedropper and some liquid tempera paint to drop paint onto paper to make a picture. Use different colors, if you like, and be sure to put the painting on display when dry.

Toothpick Painting

Toothpicks
Tempera paint, liquid
Paper
Glue

Give your child toothpicks to dip into tempera paint and use as a paintbrush. When the paint dries, she can glue the toothpicks onto her painting for a three-dimensional effect.

Paint Pen

Empty roll-on deodorant bottle
Tempera paint, liquid

To make a giant paint pen for your child, pry off the top of a roll-on deodorant bottle. Fill the bottle with liquid tempera paint, and snap on the top. Your child can use this tool to draw pictures, practice her letters and numbers, or create abstract designs.

Tennis Ball Painting

Okay, this one takes courage, but it's a lot of fun (and best done outdoors!).

Newspaper
Paper
Tennis balls
Tempera paint, liquid

Spread newspapers on the sidewalk or another firm surface, and place a large sheet of paper on the ground. Dip tennis balls, a different one for each color, into liquid tempera paint, and bounce them onto the paper for a great painting effect.

Negative Painting

Textured objects
Glue
Paper, white
Tempera paint and brush
Paintbrush or toothbrush (optional)

Gather together a collection of interesting objects, such as lace doilies, paper dolls, leaves, or letters, numbers, or shapes, cut out of cardboard. Have your child place a dab of glue on each object and stick it to a white piece of paper. Then tell her to paint over the paper and the shape. When the paint is dry, remove the shape to see the negative image. You can make a unique greeting card by folding the paper in half and painting on one side.

For a different effect, place the objects on a piece of paper and have your child spatter paint over them using a paintbrush or toothbrush. Remove the objects from the paper and show your child the negative images that appear.

Paint Blot Art

Construction paper
Tempera paint, liquid
Spoon
Rolling pin

Fold a piece of construction paper in half like a greeting card, then open it up. Using liquid tempera paints and a spoon, have your child drop different colors onto one of the inside halves of the paper. Fold the paper again with the paint on the inside, and have your child roll a rolling pin over the paper to spread the paint. Open the paper and have your child use her imagination to decide what the blot looks like. When the paint is dry, fold the paper so the paint is on the outside. Use as a unique greeting card.

Window Stenciling

Leaves in different shapes and sizes
Masking tape
Sponge
Clothespins
Tempera paint (orange, yellow, red, and brown), liquid
Newspaper

On a fall walk with your child, collect several different types and colors of leaves. At home, attach rolled pieces of masking tape to the backsides of the leaves and arrange them on the window in the way you want them to appear in stenciled form. Make sure the leaves lay flat against the glass. Dip small pieces of sponge clipped onto clothespins into liquid tempera paints in fall colors. Blot on newspaper to absorb excess paint, then lightly dab the sponge around the edge of each leaf. Use a new piece of sponge for each color. When the paint is dry, carefully remove the leaves, leaving the outlines on the window. The leaf patterns can be easily removed with window cleaner.

PRINTMAKING

Young children can experience a sense of great accomplishment with printmaking. Not only is printmaking fun, but it allows a young child to achieve an attractive reproduction of an object without a great amount of artistic skill or coordination. Through the repetition of an impression, children can develop an appreciation of texture and design.

Printmaking involves making an impression of an object onto paper or another surface. The object to be printed can be covered in paint using a brush or a paint roller, dipped into paint, or pressed on a print pad.

A print pad can be made by padding up newspaper and soaking it in liquid tempera. Or place a thin sponge in a shallow tray or small bowl and cover it with several tablespoons of paint. For some printmaking, a rubber stamp pad can also be used. To cushion the print, place a newspaper under the paper on which the impression is to be made.

Many different types of paper can be used for printing; newsprint, construction paper, and cut-open brown paper bags are some of the cheaper options. As with many of the painting projects in this chapter, you can use these printing activities to create some great, environmentally friendly gift wrap.

Fruit and Vegetable Printing

Various fruit and vegetables
Paring knife
Print pad or stamp pad
Paper

Cut fruits and vegetables into halves, quarters, circles, or any other shapes, dip into tempera paints or on a print or stamp pad, and then press onto plain or colored paper. Apples cut in half will have a star design in the middle (where the seeds are), while green peppers make a great shamrock design. Cut a potato in half and use a small paring knife to create a relief design: circles, squares, hearts, and so on. If you make letters, don't forget to carve them backwards so they will print correctly.

Playdough Printing

Playdough
Tools for making a design (pencil, bottle cap, cookie cutter,
   cooking utensils)
Print pad
Paper

Roll playdough into a ball and flatten it until it is about two
inches thick. On one side of the dough, press in a design using
a pencil, bottle cap, cookie cutter, or other cooking utensil.
Gently press the clay onto the print pad then onto paper.
Repeat using various colors and designs.

Gadget Printing

½-inch softwood cubes or matchboxes
Small objects in interesting shapes (matchsticks, string, wood
  chips, curtain rings, bottle caps, or cardboard shapes)
Glue
Print pad or rubber stamp pad
Paper

Glue interesting shapes onto half-inch softwood cubes or matchboxes; matchsticks, string, wood chips, curtain rings, keys, bottle caps, or shapes cut from cardboard are just a few examples. You can make letter or number stamps on wood cubes by drawing the image in reverse, then chipping away the surface except for the shape to be printed. Or use larger objects, such as a potato masher, fly swatter, or salt shaker. Press the object onto the print pad or rubber stamp pad and stamp it on the paper, varying colors and objects to create unique designs.

Mesh Printing

Scissors
Plastic mesh
Small foam ball
Twist-tie
Tempera paint, liquid
Shallow tray or dish
Paper

Cut out a square of plastic mesh large enough to gather
around a small foam ball. Secure the ends with a twist-tie.
Pour liquid tempera paint into a shallow tray or dish. Dip the
mesh ball into the paint, and dab the mesh onto a piece of
paper. Use different colors for a unique effect.

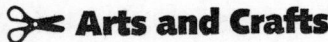

Sponge Printing

Scissors
Small thick sponges
Clothespins
Print pad
Paper

Cut sponges into various shapes. On the top of each sponge cut two slots for clothespins, making the slots about a quarter-inch deep and three-quarter-inches apart. Clip the clothespins to the top of the sponges for handles. Press the sponges onto the print pad and stamp them onto the paper. Use various shapes and colors for an interesting effect.

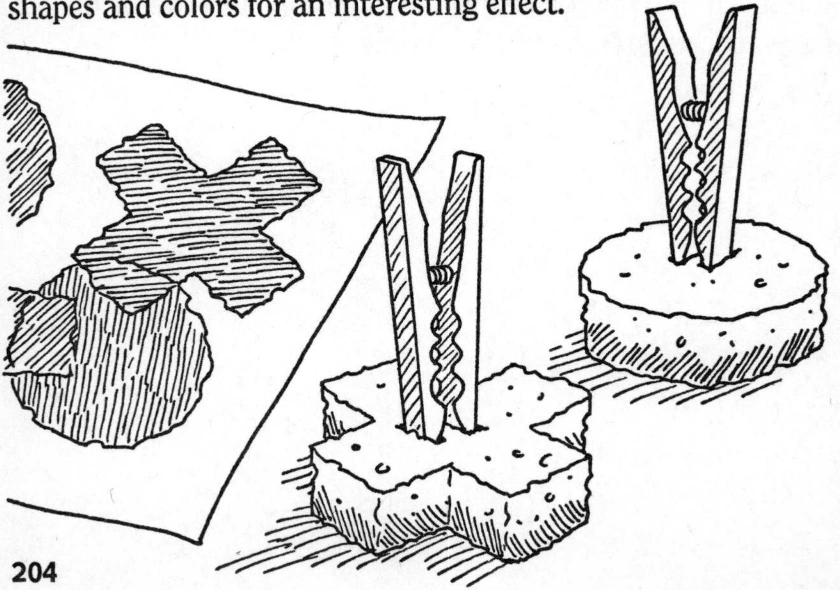

Roller Printing

Thin foam
Scissors
Glue
Empty paper towel or toilet paper roll
Tempera paint, liquid
Shallow pan
Paper or a cut-open brown paper bag

Cut out some interesting shapes from thin pieces of foam. Stars are nice, or make hearts, Christmas trees, or other season-appropriate shapes. Glue the shapes onto empty paper towel or toilet paper rolls. Pour some liquid tempera paint into a shallow pan big enough to fit the paper roll. Dip the "roller" into the paint, then roll onto a sheet of paper or cut-open brown paper bag.

For a variation on this, use a real foam paint roller. At even intervals, tie the roller with string. This will make stripes when dipped in paint and pressed on paper. Or cut chunks out of the roller to make a thick solid pattern with holes in it.

Fingerpaint Prints

Fingerpaint
Plastic tabletop
Large sheets of paper

You can purchase commercial fingerpaint, or you can make
your own using the fingerpaint recipes in Appendix A. Place a
small amount of fingerpaint onto a plastic tabletop, and have
your child mess around until her design is complete. Have her
wash and dry her hands thoroughly, then place a large sheet of
paper on top of the fingerpainting. Rub all over the back of the
paper with clean, dry hands. Slowly lift the paper off the table
and hang to dry.

Crayon Melt Prints

This activity requires the use of a food warming tray or electric griddle. Close supervision by an adult is recommended.

Food warming tray or electric griddle
Aluminum foil
Crayons
Paper
Oven mitts
Damp cloth

Cover a food warming tray or electric griddle with aluminum foil. Set on low setting and, when the tray is warm, have your child make a drawing on the foil with a crayon. The crayon will melt as you draw and produce beautiful, colorful designs. To make a print, lay a sheet of paper over the crayon design and carefully smooth the paper down with oven mitts. Lift it off and see the design transferred onto the paper. Wipe the foil clean with a damp cloth and start again for a new print.

Paper Batik

Construction paper
Crayons
Tempera paint, liquid
Paintbrush
Newspaper
Paper
Hot iron

Have your child completely color a piece of construction paper with crayons. Show her how to crumple the paper carefully into a tight ball, then gently unfold the picture and notice how the surface has cracked. Brush contrasting liquid tempera paint over the paper to create a mosaic effect. When the picture dries, place it on a sheet of newspaper and cover it with a piece of thin paper. Using a patting motion, iron the paper with a hot iron to smooth the wrinkles and to transfer the original image to the blank paper.

String Block Printing

String or rope
Small blocks of wood
Tempera paint, liquid
Shallow pan
Paper

Wrap string or rope several times around a small block of wood. Tie it in place (make sure the rope is distributed evenly over the block, not gathered in one spot). Have your child press the string block into liquid tempera paint, then press onto paper. She should move the block around in different directions and add colors to vary the design.

SCULPTING

Sculpting, creating three-dimensional structures, challenges a child's imagination. Not only is it artistic, but messing around with Super Goop and other modeling compounds can also encourage a scientific interest in your child (science begins as a "hands-on" activity).

Many materials can be used for sculpting. Your child is probably familiar with playdough and modeling clay (see Appendix A). Following are some other ideas you may want to try.

Super Goop

Saucepan
2 cups water
½ cup cornstarch
Food coloring
Mixing spoon
Ziploc bags (optional)

Boil water in a saucepan. Add cornstarch and stir until smooth. Add food coloring and stir—adjust the amount of food coloring until you get the color you want. Remove from heat and cool. Let your child squish away on the tabletop, or, for less mess (or younger children), pour the mixture into two Ziploc bags and seal. Your child can squish the bag or trace letters, numbers, or shapes on the outside of the bag.

Whipped Snow

2 cups warm water
1 cup pure laundry soap or soap flakes
Large bowl
Electric mixer
Food coloring (optional)

Put water and soap in a large bowl and beat with an electric mixer until very fluffy. Add color if desired. If you like, separate the mixture into a number of bowls, and tint each a different color. Have your child mold the fluff into shapes and allow the shapes to dry.

Homemade Silly Putty

2 parts white glue
1 part liquid starch
Small mixing bowl
Airtight container

Combine glue and starch in a bowl and mix well. Let dry until the putty is workable. You may have to add a bit more glue or starch. (This may not work well on a humid day.) Experiment! Store in an airtight container.

Plaster Hand and Footprints

Patch plaster or plaster of Paris
1¼ cups water
Tin can
Mixing spoon
Paper plates
Picture hook (optional)

To make the plaster mix, stir two cups of patch plaster or plaster of Paris and one and a quarter cups water in a tin can. The mixture should be as thick as pea soup so it can cast without air bubbles. Plaster of Paris dries in about ten to twenty minutes, while patch plaster takes twenty to forty minutes to dry.

To make a cast of your child's hand or footprint, pour one inch of plaster mix into a paper plate. Wait two minutes for plaster of Paris, six minutes for patch plaster. Have your child press her hand or foot gently into the plaster. The imprint should not go to the bottom of the plate. Hold for one to two minutes and remove. Let the imprint sit overnight, then peel the plate from the print. If you like, glue a picture hook to the back and hang the print on your child's wall.

Sugar Cube Sculpture

Sugar cubes
Glue
Styrofoam meat trays or a piece of heavy cardboard
Food coloring or tempera paint, liquid

Let your child create wonderful sculptures by gluing sugar cubes onto a Styrofoam meat tray or a piece of heavy cardboard, and also onto each other. You can color the cubes by quickly dipping them into food coloring or by lightly dabbing them with liquid tempera paint.

PAPIER-MÂCHÉ

Papier-mâché can be a very messy activity, but it is a lot of fun for children and adults alike. Papier-mâché is a special kind of paper modeling that uses paste in combination with paper or other materials, such as newsprint, paper toweling, gift wrap, crepe paper, tissue paper, construction paper, or aluminum foil. Paper can be torn into two-inch or larger squares or long strips. Torn edges glue better and result in a more interesting finished appearance.

For young children, a basic flour-and-water paste is the best bonding material to use. Begin with one cup of water; mix in about a quarter cup of flour, until the mixture is thin and runny. Stir this mixture into five cups lightly boiling water. Gently boil and stir for two to three minutes. Cool until you can dip the paper into it.

Pour the paste into a shallow tray. Dip strips of paper into the tray, or brush paste on with a paintbrush. Paste the strips over a form, such as an inflated balloon, an empty toilet paper or paper towel roll, or even crumpled newspaper. Add as many layers as you like; model the form with your fingers as you go. Tissue paper can be used as the final layer for a colorful finish.

Papier-Mâché Bracelet

Cardboard tube or baby bottle
Scissors
Papier-mâché paste
Newsprint or other paper
Colored tissue paper or paint

For this project you will need a cardboard tube large enough in diameter to slip over your child's hand. Cut one- or two-inch pieces of the tube and cover them with layers of paper and paste. Finish with brightly colored strips of tissue paper or paint. Or, instead of using a cardboard tube, use a bottle with the appropriate diameter (baby bottles work well). Grease or powder the bottle, then start with molding a layer of newsprint around the bottle. Add a layer of heavier construction paper for strength, then add an additional six layers of papier-mâché. Remove the bracelet from the bottle and finish with paint or strips of tissue paper.

Papier-Mâché Hat

Papier-mâché paste
2 large squares of wrapping paper
String
Paint

To make a fancy hat, paste together two big squares of wrapping paper with papier-mâché paste. Set this on your child's head, mold the crown of the hat, and tie a string around your child's forehead to hold the shape. After ten minutes, remove the hat, shape, let dry, and paint.

Papier-Mâché Piñata

Large inflated balloon
String
Newsprint or other paper
Papier-mâché paste
Small toys and candy
Crepe paper or tissue paper
Paints

This is a great project to make for a birthday party or other special occasion. Hang a big balloon from a string and cover it with many layers of paper and paste, leaving a hole about six inches in diameter at the top of the balloon, around the string. This will take several days to dry. When dry, pop the balloon and pour in toys and candy, then cover the opening with more paper and paste. Let dry again, then decorate the outside with fringed crepe paper or paints. Have the children try to break the piñata by taking turns swinging at it with a toy baseball bat or golf club.

CUTTING AND PASTING

Most young children gain enormous pleasure from the use of
scissors and the feel of paste. Buy your child a good pair of
child-safe scissors and teach her how to use them safety. Show
her how to keep the edges sharp by cutting sandpaper.

For paste, you can use commercial white glue or make
glue or paste using the recipes in Appendix A. Glue and paste
is best applied with a small paintbrush, although Popsicle
sticks or plastic applicators from the art store can also be
used. For variety, tint the glue with food coloring.

Keep a stack of old magazines and catalogs on hand for
cutting. An old wallpaper book is also great for all the
interesting shapes and patterns it contains. Cut out circles,
squares, rectangles, triangles, or other creative shapes, and
glue them onto construction paper to make designs and
pictures.

Chinese Lantern

Construction paper
Scissors
Glue or stapler

Fold construction paper in half lengthwise and show your child how to cut from the folded edge to within one and a half inches of the opposite side. When cuts have been made along the entire length of the paper, unfold and form into a cylinder by joining together the short uncut ends of the paper. Glue or staple another strip of construction paper for a handle.

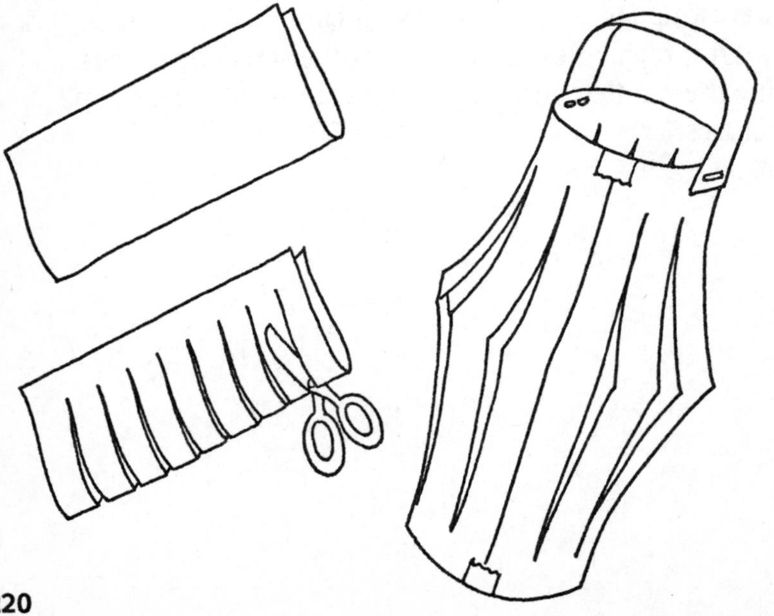

Funny Face

Old magazines
Scissors
Paper
Glue

Look through old magazines, searching for pictures of faces, and cut out as many eyes, noses, mouths, ears, and heads of hair as you can find. Mix them up and have your child piece together a funny face; then paste it onto a piece of paper.

Picture Place Mat

Family photographs
Cardboard or construction paper
Glue
Clear contact paper

Give your child the family photographs that didn't make it into your photo album. Have her glue them onto a piece of cardboard or construction paper and cover with clear contact paper. This place mat makes a great gift for Daddy, grandparents, and other family members.

Tissue Art

Glue
Paper cup or small plastic container
Water
Paintbrush
Paper
Tissue paper cut into ½-by-16-inch strips
Scissors
Sequins, beads, glitter (optional)

Pour a small amount of glue into a paper cup or small plastic container, and add about a quarter cup water to get the consistency of paint. Have your child use a paintbrush to paint the glue solution onto a piece of paper. Then, crumple up strips of brightly colored tissue paper and press them onto the paper. Use a variety of colors and add sequins, beads, and glitter for a real piece of art.

Personal Puzzle

Old magazines, catalogs, or greeting cards
Photograph of your child (optional)
Cardboard
Glue
Scissors

Cut out pictures from magazines, catalogs, or greeting cards, or use an enlarged photograph of your child. Glue the picture onto a piece of cardboard that has been cut to the same size. When dry, let your child cut the picture into pieces to create her own puzzle. Puzzles are great for helping your child recognize shapes—a prerequisite to learning letters and numbers.

Torn Tissue Design

Tissue paper
White glue
Paintbrush
White poster board
Acrylic polymer (optional)
Synthetic paintbrush (optional)

Have your child tear various colors of tissue paper into large pieces. Brush white glue thinned with water onto the back of each piece and arrange them on a piece of white poster board. Show your child how to create new colors by overlapping two pieces of different tissue paper; yellow over red makes orange, light blue over pink makes purple, and so on. To give a nice sheen to the finished product, coat it with an acrylic polymer using a synthetic paintbrush (available at an art supply store).

Circle Bear

Brown and white construction paper
Scissors
Glue
Black marker or crayon

Cut circles of brown construction paper. You will need one large circle for the body, two small circles for paws, a medium circle for the head, two half circles for feet, and two smaller half circles for ears. Show your child how to glue the circles onto white construction paper to form a bear. Your child can use a black marker or crayon to draw a face. You can also cut out small white circles to glue into place on the paws, ears, and tummy.

Gingerbread People

Thin cardboard or brown construction paper
Pen or marker
Scissors
Glue
Lace, ribbon, fabric scraps
Pieces of cereal, small candy, or licorice

Draw the outline of a gingerbread girl or boy on thin cardboard or brown construction paper. Your child can cut it out and dress it by gluing bits of lace and ribbon or scraps of fabric onto the figure. Make a face out of cereal or candy.

Shadow Silhouette

Bright light
Construction paper
Tape
Pencil
Scissors
Glue

Have your child stand sideways against a wall and shine a
bright light on her to make a profile shadow on the wall. Tape
a piece of construction paper onto the wall shadow, and trace
your child's silhouette. Have her cut it out and mount it on
another piece of construction paper in a contrasting color.

Tissue Paper Mirror

Cardboard
Scissors
Aluminum foil
Glue
Tissue paper cut into 4-inch squares

Cut cardboard into the shape of a hand mirror. Cut a piece of
aluminum foil into a corresponding shape and glue it onto
one side of the cardboard to make "glass." Have your child
crumple four-inch squares of colored tissue paper into balls
and glue them close together on the other side of the mirror
to make a flower-covered back.

Foil Wrapping Paper

Heavy-duty aluminum foil
Colored tissue paper
Acrylic polymer
Water
Synthetic paintbrush

Make your own foil wrapping paper using heavy-duty aluminum foil, tissue paper, and acrylic polymer (available at art supply stores). Tear or cut pieces of tissue paper and arrange them on the aluminum foil. Mix the acrylic polymer with a little water and brush over the tissue paper, letting it soak through. It will make the paper stick to the foil and give it a really glossy finish.

Jelly Bean Picture

Cardboard
Ornamental Frosting (see page 365)
Jelly beans

Help your child draw a picture with Ornamental Frosting on a piece of cardboard—this frosting works like glue and tastes great! Have her place jelly beans on the frosting. You can give this project a seasonal theme by using pastel jelly beans on a rabbit picture for Easter, or green jelly beans on a Christmas tree and beans of other colors for lights and decorations. Avoid using glue for this project, because your child is sure to eat the jelly beans.

Eggshell Mosaic

This is a great way to use up the remains of the Easter eggs. Your child will have a lot of fun breaking up the eggshells, and the pretty colors make a great mosaic.

Colored eggshells
Construction paper
Crayon, pen, or marker
Glue

On a piece of construction paper, have your child draw a simple design. Fill it in with glue and add the bits of colored eggshell. If you don't have colored eggshells available, dye your eggshells just as you would dye hard-boiled eggs. (See pages 287–294.)

Favorite Foods

Old magazines
Scissors
Glue
Paper plate
Pipe cleaner
Tape

Have your child cut pictures of her favorite foods from old magazines. Paste them onto a paper plate and tape a curved pipe cleaner onto the back for hanging. Or make a place mat by gluing the pictures onto a piece of construction paper and covering with clear contact paper.

CRAFTS AND OTHER FUN THINGS TO MAKE

Not only will craft projects challenge your child's imagination and artistic ability, they will fill in many hours on a rainy afternoon and help keep your child stimulated and happy. Make crafts as gifts for friends and family, or use them to brighten up your child's room and the rest of the house. Most of these projects can be made using objects found around the house or collected on your daily walks.

Styrofoam People

Styrofoam balls and blocks in different sizes
Toothpicks
Scraps of yarn and fabric
Glue
Markers or paint

Use toothpicks to join Styrofoam shapes together to form people, a snowman, animals, and so on. Glue scraps of yarn and fabric onto the Styrofoam to make hair and clothes. Use markers or paint to add faces or other details.

Cookie Cutter Cards

Construction paper
Crayon, pen, or marker
Scraps of fabric or lace, paper doilies, glitter, and stickers

Fold a piece of plain or construction paper in half to make a greeting card. Have your child trace around cookie cutters in appropriate shapes, e.g., hearts for Valentine's Day, trees or angels for Christmas. The card can then be decorated with scraps of fabric or lace, paper doilies, glitter, stickers, and so on.

Homemade Fan

Paper
Crayons or markers

Have your child draw a design on a piece of construction paper or plain paper and show her how to make a fan by folding the paper back and forth in one-inch folds. She can color one or both sides of the fan. As a variation, fold the fan first, then unfold and have your child color and decorate each panel separately.

Playdough Jewelry

Playdough
Toothpick or large, blunt needle
Clear gloss enamel or nail polish
String

Have your child roll small pieces of playdough into balls to make beads. Pierce each bead with a toothpick or large blunt needle and allow to dry for several days. Check holes after a day to see if they need repunching. When dry, coat with clear gloss enamel or nail polish to bring out the color. Thread beads onto a string and knot the ends together to create a necklace or bracelet.

Rainbow Fan

Paint sample cards
Hole punch
Paper fastener
Yarn or string

Pick up some colorful paint sample cards from your local
hardware store. Punch a hole in the center of the bottom and
top of each card. At one end, join the cards with a paper
fastener. At the other, lace yarn through the holes in each card
to form the top of a fan.

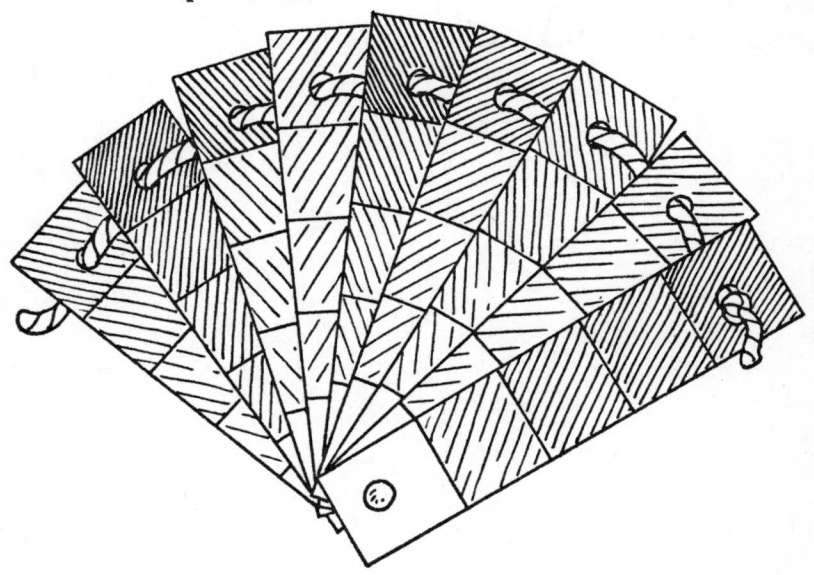

Spoon People

Wooden kitchen spoon
Glue
Yarn
Buttons
Markers

Use a wooden kitchen spoon to make a spoon person. Have your child glue yarn onto the top of the spoon to make hair and buttons to make eyes. Draw a mouth and nose with markers. Make several of these for a spoon family, and encourage your child to tell a story with these little people.

Paper Towel Art

A quick, clean alternative to "real" painting.

Paper towel
Newspaper
Food coloring or unsweetened Kool-Aid or Jell-O powder
Clean, empty salt shakers (optional)

Lay a piece of paper towel over newspaper and show your child how to drop food coloring onto the paper towel. Use different colors to make an interesting design. For variety, wet the paper towel first and lightly shake unsweetened Kool-Aid drink mix or Jell-O powder onto it. Use a variety of vivid colors and let them dry for a beautiful result. For younger children who might be tempted to dump the entire package at once, put the drink mix or Jell-O powder in a clean, empty salt shaker before using.

Framed Flowers

Flowers or leaves
Crayon shavings
Wax paper
Newspaper
Iron

Go out on a walk with your child and pick some pretty spring flowers or fall leaves. At home, make shavings of brightly colored crayons with a grater or knife. Place a piece of wax paper, wax side up, on top of several layers of newspaper on your work surface. Arrange the flowers or leaves on top of the wax paper and sprinkle with crayon shavings. Cover with another piece of wax paper, wax side down. Place several layers of newspaper on top and iron thoroughly until the crayons are melted. Hang to dry. A smaller version glued to one half of a folded piece of construction paper makes a unique and beautiful greeting card.

Binoculars

This idea may sound a bit ridiculous, but you will be amazed at how much fun a child will have with these!

Two toilet paper rolls, or a paper towel roll cut in half
Tape
Markers, crayons, stickers, and so on

Tape two toilet paper rolls together to make a pair of binoculars for your child. She can decorate them with markers, stickers, and so on, and use them to spot interesting things as you go for a walk or ride in the car.

Paper Bag Kite

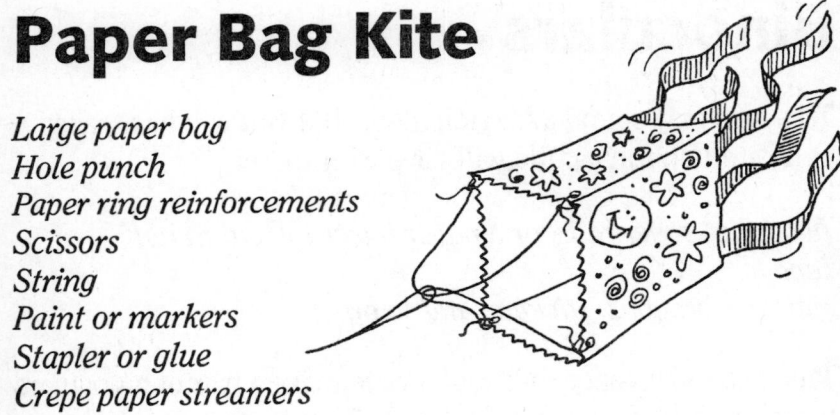

Large paper bag
Hole punch
Paper ring reinforcements
Scissors
String
Paint or markers
Stapler or glue
Crepe paper streamers

Punch a hole on each of the four corners of a large paper bag, at least one inch from the edge of the bag. Place a paper ring reinforcement on each hole. Cut two three-foot lengths of string and tie each end to a hole to form two loops. Cut another three-foot length of string and tie it through the two loops to create a handle. Have your child decorate the bag with paint or markers, and give her crepe paper streamers to glue or staple onto the bag. When your child holds onto the string and runs, the kite will fill with air and float behind her.

Coffee Can Canisters

Empty coffee cans
Paintings, drawings, or other artwork your child has made
Scissors
Glue
Clear contact paper

Use your child's artwork to create some decorative and useful canisters out of empty coffee cans. Cut the artwork to completely cover the can and glue it on, overlapping the edges. To protect the artwork, cover the outside of the can with clear contact paper. These canisters are great for holding crayons, playdough, cookie cutters, or small toys, and they make fun alternatives to gift wrap.

Wax Paper Art

Newspaper
Wax paper
Crayons
Grater or knife
Iron

Place several layers of newspaper on your work surface. Place a sheet of wax paper on top of the newspaper, wax side up. Shave, chop finely, or grate crayons onto the wax paper. Place a second sheet of wax paper, wax side down, on top of the first sheet (so that crayon pieces are in between). Cover with several layers of newspaper and iron with a hot iron until crayons are melted. Hang to dry.

Pinwheel

Plain or construction paper
Crayons, markers, glitter, stickers, and other decorative items
Scissors
Tape
Paper fastener
Cardboard cut into a small circle
Straw, wooden dowel, or unsharpened pencil

Have your child decorate a square piece of paper with crayons, markers, paint, glitter, stickers, and so on. Mark the center of the square and cut from each corner into the center, stopping one inch from the center. Fold every other point into the center and tape; make sure the decorated side of the paper is on the outside. Push a paper fastener through a small circular piece of cardboard, then through the center of the pinwheel. Fasten around a straw, wooden dowel, or unsharpened pencil.

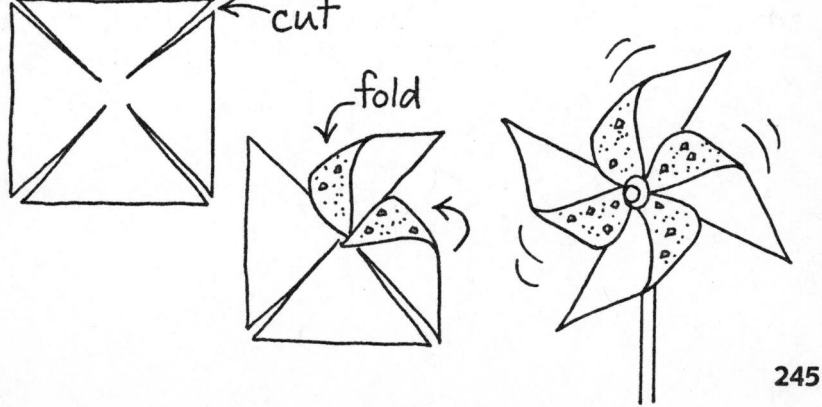

cut

fold

Waxed Leaves

Leaves
Newspaper
Wax paper
Iron

On a fall walk with your child, collect a variety of types and colors of leaves. At home, cover your ironing board with several layers of newspaper, then place a sheet of wax paper on top. Have your child arrange her leaves on top of the wax paper. Place a second sheet of wax paper over the leaves. Cover with a layer of newspaper and place a medium-hot iron on top. Hold the iron in place for about thirty seconds. Then move the iron to another section of the wax paper. Continue until all areas of the wax paper have been heated. Lift off the paper and remove the leaves. They should be waxed enough to retain their shape. Arrange them in a vase or use them in some other artwork.

Pasta Picture

Pasta in various shapes
Paper plate or piece of cardboard
Glue
Tempera paints
Paintbrush

Glue various shapes of pasta onto a paper plate or a piece of cardboard, and paint the pasta with tempera paints. If you prefer, dye the pasta ahead of time by mixing half a cup of alcohol with food coloring. The larger the pasta, the longer it will take to absorb the color. Dry the pasta on newspaper covered with wax pape. When the pasta is dry, have your child use it to create a pasta picture.

Party Hats

Construction paper
Crayons, markers, stickers, and other decorative items
Tape or stapler
Scissors
Elastic thread or ribbon

Let your child decorate a piece of construction paper with crayons, markers, stickers, and so on. Fold the paper into a cone shape, tape or staple the overlapping edges together, and cut the bottom edge so it is even. Staple a length of elastic thread or ribbon to each side for hat straps.

Noodle Necklace

Macaroni noodles
String
Tempera paints
Paintbrush

Make a noodle necklace by threading macaroni noodles on a string. Knot the ends together and paint the noodles with tempera paints. Let the necklace dry thoroughly before letting your child wear her creation.

Modern Art

Piece of cardboard or paper plate
Glue or paste
Small household items (cereal, buttons, macaroni, sequins,
  cut-up straws, plastic jug lids, and so on)

Give your child a strong piece of cardboard or a paper plate, some glue, and small items of different sizes, shapes, and textures: cereal, buttons, macaroni, sequins, cut-up straws, plastic juice jug lids, and so on. Let your child create her own version of modern art.

Egg Carton Butterfly

Cardboard egg carton
Scissors
Tempera paints
Paintbrush
Pipe cleaners
Construction paper
Markers
Stapler

Cut an egg carton in half lengthwise, then cut one of the halves in half again, lengthwise. Turn one of the halves upside down and paint with tempera paint. Attach pipe cleaners to the head for feelers. Cut wings from construction paper and decorate with paint or markers; staple to the side of the carton. Use your imagination to make variations; for example, use one cup of the carton to make a turtle or a ladybug, use three cups to make a bumblebee, or use a full half carton to make a caterpillar.

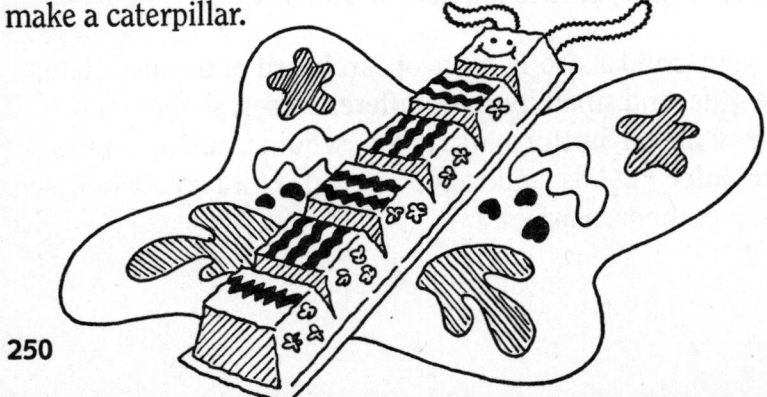

Paper Bag Vest

Large brown paper bag
Scissors
Paint

Make a vest from a brown paper bag by cutting a head hole, arm holes, and a fringe along the bottom. Your child can paint and decorate the vest. When the vest is dry, your child can wear it.

Napkin Rings

Empty paper towel or toilet paper rolls
Scissors
Crayons, paints, stickers, or glitter

Make napkin rings for a special occasion or to give as a gift. Cut empty paper towel or toilet paper rolls into one-and-a-half-inch pieces. Have your child decorate them with crayons, paints, stickers, or glitter.

Picture Frame

Baby food or other jar lid, or metal lid from frozen juice cans
Photograph
Pen
Scissors
Glue
Ribbon
Magnets

Place a jar lid or the metal lid from a frozen juice can on the photograph you wish to frame and trace around it. Cut out the photo and glue it inside the lid. If you use a jar lid, tie a ribbon around the outside of the lid. Glue a magnet to the back of the lid and place it on the refrigerator.

Feather Headband

Construction paper or poster board
Scissors
Stapler
Glue
Feathers (optional)
Markers or crayons (optional)

Cut a strip of brown construction paper or poster board about one and a half inches wide. Measure the length by placing the headband around your child's head and stapling the ends together to fit snugly. Cut several feather shapes out of colored construction paper (or gather some real feathers on a walk) and glue to the headband. Your child can draw a design on the headband with markers or crayons if she wishes.

Picture Soap

Bar of soap
Glue
Photograph or other picture
Canning wax
Small empty can
Pan
Hot water
Paintbrush

Glue a photograph or any other picture onto a bar of soap.
Melt canning wax in a small empty can in a pan of hot water.
To waterproof the picture, dip a paintbrush in the melted wax
and paint it over the picture. Your child can take a bath with
her special soap or save it to give as a gift.

Egg Carton Flowers

Empty egg cartons
Scissors
Paint, markers, or crayons
Paintbrush
Pipe cleaner
Green construction paper
Glue

Cut apart an egg carton into individual sections and have your child paint the sections with a variety of colors. (Markers or crayons can also be used.) Poke a pipe cleaner through the bottom of each section to make a stem. Cut leaf shapes out of green construction paper and glue them onto the pipe cleaners. Several colorful flowers in a bud vase make a great gift or a decorative table centerpiece.

Parade Shaker

Paper towel roll
Stapler
Crepe paper
Scissors

Decorate an empty paper towel roll by stapling several twelve-inch strips of crepe paper to each end of the roll. Cut each strip into thirds, lengthwise, to make each strip into three narrow strips. Scrunch each strip with your fingers to make the shaker look fuller. Let your little one have her own parade by holding onto the roll and shaking the streamers. If you use toilet paper rolls, attach the streamers to only one end, so your child has plenty of room to hold onto the shaker.

Bird Feeder

Pine cone
String
Peanut butter
Knife for spreading
Bird seed

Make your own bird feeder with peanut butter, a pine cone, and bird seed. Tie a string around the top of the pine cone under the ridges, so the string stays in place, and knot it, leaving enough string for hanging. Thoroughly cover the pine cone with peanut butter, then roll it in bird seed. Hang the feeder outside near a window and your child can watch the birds eat.

Paper Doll Chain

Large sheets of paper or newspaper
Scissors
Crayons or markers

Fold a large sheet of paper like a fan (newspaper, a cut-open
paper bag, or computer paper works well). The fan folds
should be as wide as you want your dolls to be. Draw a doll
shape with arms and legs extended from the body, so that the
hands and feet fall on the folds. Cut out the doll shape, taking
care not to cut through the folds at the hands and feet; if you
cut through, you will end up with a lot of single paper dolls
instead of a chain. Unfold the chain and let your child decorate
each doll with crayons or markers. With a little practice, your
child will soon be able to make a doll chain on her own.

Rock Art

Rocks
Glue
Paint
Paintbrush
Playdough or fabric scraps, ribbon, or lace

Make rock people or rock animals by gluing together rocks you have collected on walks. Your child can then paint her rock art and add accessories made out of playdough or fabric scraps, ribbon, or lace.

Toy Boats

Styrofoam meat trays
Straw
White construction paper
Scissors
Tape

Make toy sailboats with clean Styrofoam meat trays. Insert a straw into the tray for the mast. Cut triangular sails from white construction paper and tape to the straw. Your child can sail her boat in a bathtub, a swimming pool, or a tub of water.

Coat Rack

Four eight-penny nails
1-foot length of 1-by-2-inch wood
Hammer
Tempera paint, markers, or crayons

This is something your child can make that is useful, and it
makes a good gift for someone special. Show your child how
to hammer a row of four eight-penny nails into a one-foot
length of one-by-two-inch wood. The wood can then be
painted with tempera paints, markers, or crayons. Be sure to
display this in a prominent place.

Straw Holders

This is a great project for a special occasion or holiday, or just to make any day special.

Thin cardboard
Scissors
Hole punch
Crayons, markers, or stickers
Straws

Use thin cardboard (a paper plate or file folder works well) to cut out a square, circle, or special shape (like a heart for Valentine's Day). Use a hole punch to make a hole at the top and bottom of your cutout, then have your child decorate the cutout with crayons, markers, or stickers. Insert a drinking straw into one hole and out the other. Your child can then use this to drink her favorite beverage.

Tall Trees

Newspaper
Tape
Scissors
Empty toilet paper or paper towel roll
Piece of heavy cardboard

Roll up the long side of one sheet of newspaper and tape it closed. Cut one end of the roll into a fringe using long snips, fairly close together. Reach inside the fringed end of the roll and carefully pull out the center to make the tree spiral up until it's tall. The fringes become the leaves of the tree; curl them or dress them up with paper flowers. To display your tree, stand it on an empty toilet paper or paper towel roll taped to a heavy cardboard base.

CHAPTER 9

Birthdays and Holidays

"The first holiday may have been invented to celebrate fertility
or planting or harvest, but we're sure a mother was behind it.
Even then she must have known that nothing could cure her
day-to-day drudgery as well as a holiday or brighten the eye of
a small child so quickly."
—*Marguerite Kelly and Elia Parsons*

Nothing can disrupt your daily routine like a holiday, yet
nothing is quite so important. Mothers and small children
alike often need the lift of a special day on which we can focus
energy and attention. In addition to celebrating birthdays and
traditional holidays, make the most of each small victory and
accomplishment. You don't have to go all out all the time; put
a candle on the dinner table and use your best china to make
even an ordinary day extraordinary. Most of the fun and
excitement comes from the anticipation that builds as the
celebration draws near, so be sure to allow your child to take
part in the planning and preparation for each festivity.

BIRTHDAY CELEBRATIONS

For the first few years of your child's life, a family dinner complete with birthday cake and candles is usually sufficient for a birthday celebration. But somewhere around the third or fourth year, your child will probably want to invite a few friends over for a "real" birthday party. This will usually be about two hours long and consist mainly of eating and opening gifts. Keep the food simple; sandwiches, pizza, hot dogs, carrot sticks, fruit, juice, and chocolate milk are some suggestions. Older children will enjoy a few simple games, such as London Bridge, Pin the Tail on the Donkey, Follow the Leader, Red Light/Green Light, or Simon Says.

If you really want to go all out and organize a theme party for your child, many excellent birthday party books are available in bookstores or at your local library. In fact, Meadowbrook publishes a number of great books for kids' parties and holiday celebrations, such as Penny Warner's *Kids' Party Games and Activities, Kids' Pick-A-Party Book, Kids' Party Cookbook,* and *Kids' Holiday Fun.* (Take a look at the order form in the back of this book for more party and activity books.)

If you find the commercialism of even a small child's party appalling, you may want to consider asking parents to spend not more than a few dollars on a present. You can also be good to the environment and avoid spending a small fortune on matching hats, plates, cups, napkins, and tablecloth by using brightly colored linen and unbreakable plates. Have each child make his own party hat with construction paper, markers, stickers, and glitter (see Chapter 8) and substitute a small, wrapped gift for each child in place of a goodie bag (or dispense with this custom altogether). Store-bought thank-you notes for gifts received can be replaced with your child's original artwork.

Birthday Time Capsule

Envelope
Writing paper
Pen

This is a wonderful tradition for young and old alike. Each birthday person prepares information to be put into their "time capsule." Ask questions of young children and write down their responses. You may want to ask about favorite foods, songs, activities, friends, and so on. Ask what your child looks forward to over the year, and what he expects life to be like next year on his birthday. When everything is written down, place the paper in an envelope labeled with the birthday person's name and the Date to be Opened (next year's birthday). You'll all have a lot of fun when the time capsule is opened.

Video Time Capsule

Video camera
Videotape

If you have access to a video camera, consider taping your Birthday Time Capsule instead of writing it down. Ask questions of younger children. Older children may enjoy just talking about themselves and their day-to-day life. Once the time capsule is taped, put the tape away and don't watch it until the following year on your child's birthday. If you do this for more than one child, use a different tape for each. Add a new segment each year, keeping the previous ones, as well. Over the years, you will be able to watch your child grow up on his time capsule tape.

Super Chocolate Birthday Cake

This chocolate cake is quick and easy to make, and it is absolutely delicious. After the cake is baked and cooled, insert foil-wrapped coins into one of the layers before frosting. When cutting the cake, be sure each child receives a piece with a coin in it. You may not want to include coins in a cake for very young children because of the danger of choking.

2 cups white sugar
6 tablespoons butter
2 eggs, beaten
1 cup cocoa
Boiling water
1 teaspoon soda
1 cup boiling water
2 cups flour
2 teaspoons baking powder
2 8- or 9-inch cake pans, greased

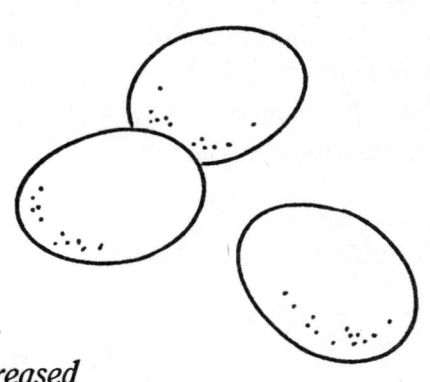

1. Preheat the oven to 350 degrees.
2. Cream sugar and butter; add beaten eggs.
3. Add enough boiling water to the cocoa to make 2 cups of liquid.

4. Add the cocoa liquid to the sugar mixture.
5. Mix soda and 1 cup boiling water, and add to the sugar/cocoa mixture.
6. Add flour and baking powder, mix well, and pour into 2 greased cake pans. Bake for 30 minutes.

Fudgy Chocolate Frosting

This recipe frosts one two-layer 8- or 9-inch cake.

3 tablespoons butter, melted
¼ cup cocoa
¼ cup milk
½ teaspoon vanilla
2 cups powdered sugar, sifted

1. Combine melted butter with cocoa.
2. Blend in milk, vanilla, and sifted icing sugar until smooth.

NEW YEAR'S DAY

The beginning of a new year is a time for a fresh start, a time for new beginnings. Whether you celebrate with a traditional family dinner or eat take-out Chinese food, the arrival of a new year is indeed an occasion worth noting.

New Year's Day is often the time we assess ourselves and set goals for our future. Consider adapting the Birthday Time Capsule or Video Time Capsule ideas (pages 266–267) for New Year's. Tape- or video-record or write down each family member's resulutions and hopes for the new year to begin a New Year's tradition for your family that you and your child will cherish for years to come.

Friends Far & Near

Christmas cards you have received
Basket

After Christmas is over, place the Christmas cards you received into a basket and set it on your table. Starting in January, take one card out of the basket each day and talk about that person or family with your child. If prayers are a part of your child's bedtime routine, this is a good way to include someone special each night.

VALENTINE'S DAY

Valentine's Day is the day to celebrate love. Start your preparations several weeks in advance as you make heart-shaped cookies, cards, and valentine crafts. On February 14th, dress the whole family in red, and put your heart-shaped cookie cutter to work for toast, sandwiches, apples, cheese, and Finger Jell-O (page 85). A small Valentine's party can be a simple and fun way to celebrate this special day.

Valentine Chain

Construction paper in red, white, and pink
Glue or paste

Cut strips of red, white, and pink construction paper, three to
four inches long and one-half to one-inch wide. Give the strips
to your child and have him form a circle with one strip, gluing
the ends together. Take the next strip and loop it through the
first circle, again gluing the ends together. Tell your child to
make a chain as long as he wants. Use it to decorate doorways,
walls, and so on.

Valentine Place Mat

Valentines your child has received
Construction paper or light cardboard
Glue or paste
Clear contact paper

Have your child glue his favorite valentines onto a large piece
of construction paper or light cardboard. Cover this collage
with clear contact paper to make a place mat.

Heart People

Construction paper in red, white, and pink
Glue or paste

Using red, white, and pink construction paper, trace and cut
hearts, ranging in size from two to six inches. Glue the hearts
together in different combinations to form heart people, using
large hearts for heads and bodies, smaller ones for arms, legs,
and so on. You can also try making heart animals.

Valentine Mobile

Valentines your child has received
Hole punch
Thread or yarn
Coat hanger

Have your child punch holes in his valentines, thread them
onto a piece of thread or yarn, and hang them from a coat
hanger to create a mobile. Hang the finished mobile from a
curtain rod.

Heart Window Decorating

Plain or construction paper
Scissors
Can of spray-on artificial snow

Fold several pieces of paper in half and cut out heart shapes in
varying sizes. The pieces of paper out of which the hearts have
been cut will serve as stencils. Tape them to the window in an
interesting arrangement and spray with artificial snow.
Remove the stencils to see the heart shapes on the window.

Heart Necklace

Plain or construction paper
Scissors
Tempera paints, liquid
Hole punch
Yarn
Photo of your child (optional)
Glue (optional)

Cut a heart shape as large as your child's hand out of plain or construction paper. Dip his hand in liquid tempera paint and press it on the paper. When the paint is dry, punch a hole in the top of the heart, and string yarn through it to make a necklace. Write a valentine's message on it, and glue a picture of your child on the other side, if you wish. Send or give the heart necklace to a special friend or relative.

Laced Heart

Poster board or heavy construction paper in valentine colors
    (white, pink, red, purple)
Hole punch
Tape
Ribbon in contrasting colors
Photo of your child (optional)
Glue (optional)
Magnet (optional)

Cut a large heart shape out of poster board or heavy construction paper. Punch an even number of holes around the outside edge of the heart. Tape one end of a ribbon between two holes, leaving an inch or two free to make a bow later, and show your child how to weave the ribbon through the holes, starting at either the bottom or top of the heart. Tie the ends in a bow. Help your child write a valentine's message on the heart. If you like, glue a photo of your child to the front of the heart and a magnet to the back.

ST. PATRICK'S DAY

Whether or not St. Patrick's Day is a big deal in your family, this holiday can help break up the monotony of the last days of winter. Dress in green and invite a few friends over for a small St. Patrick's Day celebration. Make Green Hats (page 279) together and play a few simple games. Serve green Finger Jell-O (page 85) and cupcakes or sugar cookies with green icing (or decorate them as a party activity). Color white grape juice green with a drop or two of food coloring, or serve limeade or green Kool-Aid. Wind up the day with your own St. Patrick's Day parade, wearing homemade hats and marching to the beat of drums (coffee cans or other large cans with lids), a Pie Plate Tambourine (page 152), or other homemade rhythm instruments.

Green Hats

Green paint
16-by-20-inch sheets of newspaper
1-by-2-inch piece of sponge
Plastic lids (for paint)

Fold sheets of newspaper in half, short end to short end. Fold the top corners (folded end) over so they meet in the center. Fold up the bottom edges so they meet the folded edges. Pour a small amount of paint in a plastic lid, dip the sponge in the paint, and let your child decorate the hat.

Hide the Shamrock

While this game works best with a few children, you can still play when there's just the two of you.

Green construction paper
Scissors

Cut a shamrock out of green construction paper. Choose a child to be "it." While other children hide their eyes, "it" hides the shamrock within a designated area. Everyone then opens their eyes and tries to find the shamrock. The finder gets to be "it" for the next round.

EASTER

Easter is the traditional Christian holiday that celebrates the resurrection of Jesus Christ. It is also a time to celebrate the coming of spring and all the joyous signs of new life. Consider holding a small Easter party for your child and a few friends. Make some Easter Bunny Ears and decorate eggs with your guests. Have an informal Easter parade with decorated wagons and tricycles. An Easter egg or candy hunt can be held either indoors or out, depending on the weather. Remember that children enjoy the planning and anticipation, so start your Easter crafts and activities early.

Paper Plate Easter Bunny

Large paper plate
Small paper plate
Glue
Stapler (optional)
Pink construction paper
Scissors
Crayons or markers
Cotton ball

Glue a small paper plate to a large paper plate to form the head and body of a bunny. Cut out bunny ears from pink construction paper and glue or staple to the head. Draw the bunny face with crayons or markers, and glue a cotton ball on the back for a tail.

Easter Bunny Ears

Construction paper in white and pink
Scissors
Glue
Stapler

Use white and pink construction paper to cut out bunny-ear shapes—two white and two pink, the pink being slightly smaller. Glue the pink ears onto the white ears. Glue the ears onto a long strip of construction paper, measure to fit your child's head, and staple the ends together to form a headband.

Easter Grass

Large Easter basket
Pan, large enough to hold the basket
Wheat seeds (about 1 pound)
Vermiculite (about 1 pound)
Plastic wrap

Grow a miniature meadow right in your own Easter basket.
About a week before Easter, line a large Easter basket with
plastic wrap and fill with vermiculite up to two inches below
the rim. Sprinkle the wheat seeds on top of the vermiculite,
set the basket in the sink, and add water until the seed bed is
moist. You won't have to water it again before Easter. Set the
basket in a pan and place it in filtered sunlight. Cover loosely
with plastic wrap to keep moist; remove the plastic after two
days. The wheat will begin to sprout during the next few days,
and by Easter morning, you will have real Easter grass for
hiding your Easter eggs.

Easter Bunny Mask

Paper plate
Scissors
Pink construction paper
Glue
Pink or white pipe cleaners
Yarn
Hole punch

Turn a paper plate into a bunny mask. Hold the plate against your child's face and mark where the eyes and nose holes should be. Cut out the holes for the eyes and nose. Cut out bunny ears from pink construction paper and glue to the plate. Use pipe cleaners for whiskers. Punch a hole on each side of the plate, and attach two pieces of yarn on both sides to tie the mask onto your little bunny's head.

Papier-Mâché Easter Egg

Papier-Mâché Paste (see page 363)
Pie tin
Balloon
Tape
1-inch torn strips of newspaper or paper towel
Paint
Paintbrushes
Colored tissue paper (optional)
Shellac

Mix up some Papier-Mâché Paste and put it in a pie tin. Inflate a balloon and tape it to the top of the table. Dip strips of newspaper in the paste and place them on the balloon, overlapping edges slightly. Cover the balloon completely and let dry. Have your child decorate the covered balloon by painting an Easter egg design, or cover the balloon egg with a layer of tissue paper in pastel Easter colors. Finish with shellac for a shiny, glazed effect.

Egg Decorating

There are many ways to decorate an Easter egg without using commercially prepared egg dyes. You can make your own dye with food coloring or vegetables, or you can make pretty eggs using crayons, paint, fabric, yarn, seeds, and other materials to create different effects.

If you are using hard-boiled eggs, keep them refrigerated. Do not eat them if they are not refrigerated or have been sprayed with acrylic. If you are creating special works of art, use blown eggs instead of hard-boiled. Blown eggs are more fragile, and probably not a good idea for really young children, but you can keep them from year to year.

To blow an egg, poke a small hole at each end of the egg with a large needle. Push the needle inside the egg and twist until the yoke is broken. Hold the egg over a bowl and blow hard through the hole at the top until the shell is empty. Rinse the eggshells well and allow to dry completely before decorating. (Save the raw eggs and scramble them for breakfast, or do some baking with your child.)

Once you get going, you'll come up with your own ideas. Here are just a few to get you started.

Natural Egg Dye

Saucepans, 1 for each color
Water, ½ cup for each saucepan
Various food and plant items
Strainer
Hard-boiled or blown eggs
Slotted spoon
Cooking oil
Soft cloth

Pour half a cup of water into each saucepan and add cut-up
fruit, vegetables, or plants (try carrots, blueberries, grass, and
coffee). Bring to a boil and simmer until the water turns the
color you want. Remove from heat and strain; reserve the
water. When the water cools, add eggs and allow to sit in the
water until they turn the desired color. Remove with a slotted
spoon and allow to air dry. Polish dry eggs with a small amount
of cooking oil and a soft cloth.

Crepe Paper Egg Dye

Crepe paper, variety of colors
Hot water
Small bowls or cups, 1 for each color
Hard-boiled or blown eggs
Slotted spoon
Cooking oil
Soft cloth

Soak crepe paper in hot water in a small bowl or cup, one color of crepe paper per container. Add eggs and allow to sit in the water until they turn the desired color. Remove with a slotted spoon and allow to air dry. Polish dry eggs with a small amount of cooking oil and a soft cloth.

Food Coloring Egg Dye

Small bowls or cups, 1 for each color
Food coloring, ¼ teaspoon for each color
Hot water, ¾ cup for each color
White vinegar, 1 tablespoon for each color
Hard-boiled or blown eggs
Slotted spoon
Cooking oil
Soft cloth

For each color, measure a quarter teaspoon of food coloring into a small bowl or cup. Add three-quarter cup hot water and one tablespoon white vinegar to each color. Add eggs and allow to sit in the water until they turn the desired color. Remove with a slotted spoon and allow to air dry. Polish dry eggs with a small amount of cooking oil and a soft cloth.

Marble Eggs

Grater
Wax paper or newspaper
Crayon stubs
Large glass jar
Hot water
Hard-boiled or blown eggs
Slotted spoon
Empty egg carton
Clear acrylic spray (optional)

Grate peeled crayon stubs over wax paper or newspaper. Fill a large glass jar with very hot water. Drop pinches of grated crayon into the water and add an egg as soon as the crayon begins to melt. Twirl the egg in the water with a slotted spoon; the wax will make a design on the egg. Carefully remove the egg from the water with a slotted spoon and set it in an upside-down egg carton to dry. Spray with clear acrylic when the wax is dry, if desired.

Sponge-Painted Eggs

Newspaper
Hard-boiled or blown eggs
Egg cups
Tempera paints, liquid
Paper cups, 1 for each color
Small pieces of sponge or foam
Spring-type clothespins, 1 for each color
Clear acrylic spray (optional)

Cover your work surface with newspaper. Place eggs in egg
cups. Partially fill paper cups with liquid tempera paint. Clip
pieces of sponge to clothespins and dip them into the paper
cups, using the clothespins as handles. Lightly dab the sponges
over the top half of the eggs and let dry. Turn the eggs over
and repeat. Let the eggs dry completely. If you use blown eggs,
spray them with clear acrylic for a permanent finish.

Dip and Dye Eggs

Hard-boiled eggs
Masking tape
Egg dyes in a variety of colors
Slotted spoon
Cooking oil
Soft cloth

Stick a pattern of masking tape on hard-boiled eggs. Dip them in a natural or commercial egg dye and leave them until they reach the desired color. Remove the eggs with a slotted spoon and allow them to air dry. Remove the masking tape when the eggs are completely dry. Leave the masked areas white, or dip the eggs again in a lighter dye. Polish the finished eggs with a small amount of cooking oil and a soft cloth.

Waxed Eggs

Hard-boiled eggs
Clear crayons
Egg dyes in a variety of colors
Slotted spoon
Oven
Paper towel
Cooking oil
Soft cloth

Draw a heavy crayon pattern on hard-boiled eggs and dip
them in a natural or commercial egg dye in a dark color.
Leave them in until they reach the desired color. Remove eggs
with a slotted spoon and place them in a 200-degree oven for a
few minutes to melt the crayon. Wipe with a paper towel and
dip again in a lighter color to fill in the pattern drawn with the
crayon. Polish the finished eggs with a small amount of
cooking oil and a soft cloth.

FOURTH OF JULY

The Fourth of July celebrates the anniversary of the Declaration of Independence in 1776, and so this holiday is America's birthday. Whether you celebrate with a patriotic parade or a picnic at the park, a day at the beach or a traditional family barbecue, be sure your child knows why the nation celebrates this day. Fly the flag proudly, decorate and dress with a red, white, and blue theme, bake a birthday cake and sing "Happy Birthday, United States." Your family's Fourth of July traditions and celebrations can help your children feel proud of their country.

Use your imagination to adapt some of the activities in this book for your Fourth of July celebrations. Make a birthday card for the United States. Bake star-shaped sugar cookies or cupcakes and decorate them with red, white, and blue icing. Join layers of strawberry and blueberry Jell-O with whipped cream to make red, white, and blue star-shaped Finger Jell-O (page 85). Make a fireworks painting (see Air Painting, page 188). Sing "Yankee Doodle" and march around your house or yard with a homemade drum. Have fun!

United States Flag

As you work to make this United States flag, tell your child what the colors and shapes represent.

Red and blue paper
Scissors
Glue
Large white paper
Star stickers
Dowel
Tape

Help your child tear or cut a large blue square and strips of red paper. Glue the strips and square onto white paper to make a flag. Stick stars on the blue square. Tape the flag to a dowel and fly the flag proudly!

Red, White, and Blue Salad

This one your child can do himself very little help.

Strawberries
Blueberries
Bananas

Wash and hull strawberries, wash blueberries, and peel and slice bananas. Mix all the ingredients and serve.

HALLOWEEN

While many people choose to celebrate Halloween without its traditional ghoulish emphasis, this holiday still provides an excuse for a good costume party. Our children dress in fun, nonscary costumes, and we carve a pumpkin with a big, happy face. We attend a party with a "Fall Carnival" theme where we eat, play games, and come home with enough candy to last six months.

Regardless of how you celebrate this occasion, here are some fun activities for you and your child to try.

Halloween Chain

Scissors
Black and orange construction paper
Glue or paste

Here's a variation on the traditional Christmas tree decoration.
Cut strips of black and orange construction paper, three to
four inches long and one-half to one inch wide. Have your
child form a circle with one strip, gluing the ends together.
Take the next strip and loop it through the first circle, again
gluing the ends together. Tell your child to continue looping
and gluing to make a chain as long as he wants. Use the chain
to decorate doorways, walls, windows, and so on.

Baked Pumpkin Seeds

Pumpkin seeds
Cookie sheet
Salt

As you prepare your Thanksgiving or Halloween pumpkin,
save and dry the seeds. Spread dried seeds on a cookie sheet,
salt, and quickly broil them until lightly browned. Have your
child count them into groups of two, three, four, and so on,
before eating them.

Pom-Pom Spider

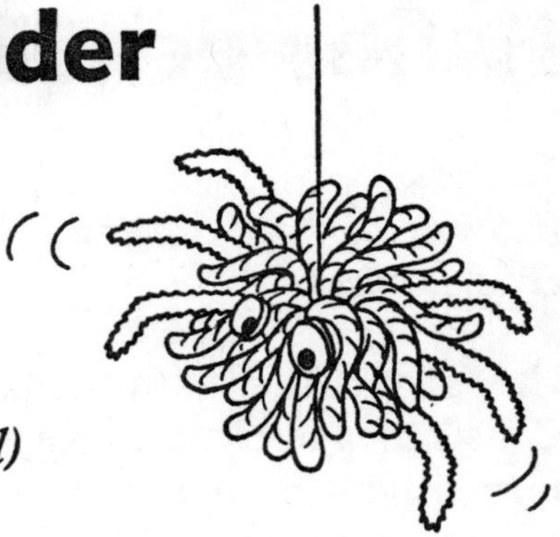

Black yarn
Small square of cardboard
Scissors
Black pipe cleaners
Googly eyes (optional)
Red construction paper (optional)
Glue (optional)

Wind black yarn around a small square of cardboard, top to bottom, until the cardboard is very heavily and snugly covered. Tie a small piece of yarn securely around the middle of the yarn and the cardboard. (This piece should be tied fairly tightly, but not knotted, as it will be tightened after the cardboard is removed.) Using scissors, cut the yarn horizontally at both ends of the cardboard. Remove the cardboard, then tighten and knot the piece of yarn in the middle; it now forms the center of the pom-pom. Insert three pipe cleaners into the knotted center, and bend to form legs. You may have to trim the yarn to form a nice, even ball. Glue on googly eyes, if you like, or cut eyes out of red construction paper and glue them onto the pom-pom. Use thread or yarn to hang your spider from the doorway or in the window.

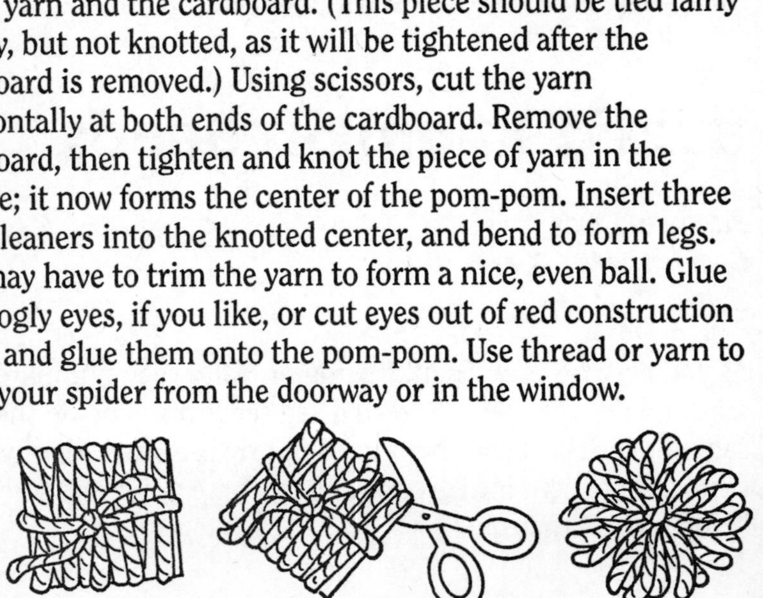

Glowing Pumpkin Drawing

Construction paper
Orange and black crayons
Black (or other contrasting color) tempera paint and brush
Varnish (optional)

Using crayons, help your child draw an outline of a pumpkin on a piece of construction or other paper. He should press hard, and fill in the outline with plenty of thick coloring. Then have him paint the picture with black (or other contrasting color) tempera paint. Since wax repels water, the colored areas will resist the paint and the painting will "glow." For a really dramatic effect, use fluorescent crayons, and finish with a coat of varnish.

Egg Carton Spider

Black tempera paint, markers, or crayons
Cardboard egg carton
Scissors
Black pipe cleaners
Red construction paper
Glue
Thread or yarn

Using paint, markers, or crayons, color the cup sections of an egg carton. If using paint, wait until the paint dries, then cut the egg cups apart. Push pipe cleaner legs into each egg cup and bend them so they look like spiders' legs. Cut red eyes from construction paper and glue them onto the cups. Use thread or yarn to hang your spiders from the doorway or in the window.

THANKSGIVING

While it is traditional to celebrate the harvest with a huge meal of roast turkey and all the trimmings, this year try to emphasize the "giving" in Thanksgiving. Talk with your child about all that you have for which you are thankful. This is an ideal time to share your wealth with others and to encourage a giving spirit in your child. Consider the following activities: Collect food in your neighborhood and take it to a local food bank; do some special baking and take the goodies to a nursing home or to a house-bound neighbor; take some good, usable clothing and toys to a local relief agency; invite someone who is alone to share your Thanksgiving celebration.

Thanksgiving Tree

Construction paper in fall colors
Poster board or cardboard
Scissors
Markers
Glue or paste
Old catalogs or magazines (optional)

Cut leaf shapes out of colored construction paper. You can draw the shapes on paper and have your child cut them out, or make a leaf pattern your child can trace himself. Draw a tree trunk and branches on a piece of cardboard or poster board. Ask your child to name things for which he is thankful and write them on each leaf (or use pictures cut from old magazines or catalogs). Have your child glue the leaves or pictures onto the branches. Display the tree in a prominent place as a reminder of your many blessings.

Thanksgiving Can

Index cards or small pieces of paper
Old magazines (optional)
Glue or paste
Empty coffee can

Several weeks before Thanksgiving, ask your child to tell you
for what he is thankful. On index cards or strips of paper, write
down what he tells you. (Or have your child search through
old magazines for appropriate pictures he can cut out and
glue onto index cards.) Place the cards inside an empty coffee
can. At bedtime, breakfast, or quiet time, have your child
reach into the can and remove one card, then talk about what
is on the card and why he is thankful for it.

Thanksgiving Place Mat

Old magazines
Construction paper or light cardboard
Glue or paste
Clear contact paper

Give your child old magazines and have him cut out things for which he is thankful. Let him glue them onto a piece of cardboard or construction paper. Cover the artwork with clear contact paper to create a Thanksgiving place mat.

Thanksgiving Place Cards

Yellow construction paper
Brown tempera paint, liquid
Pen or marker

Fold a piece of yellow construction paper in half. Dip your child's palm into liquid brown tempera paint and carefully print it on the paper. When the paint dries, make the print look like a turkey: Use a pen or marker to add legs, an eye, a beak, and a wattle (the folds of loose red flesh under a turkey's throat). Print a name next to the turkey and use it on the Thanksgiving dinner table as a place card.

Paper Plate Turkey

Paper plate
Brown paint or crayon
Construction paper in various colors
Glue or paste
Markers or crayons

Have your child color a paper plate with brown paint or crayons. Cut feathers out of colored construction paper, and glue them to the edge of the plate. Cut out a head, a neck, and feet, and glue them to the plate. Draw a turkey face with markers or crayons.

CHRISTMAS

Christmas—a time when Christians the world over traditionally celebrate the birth of the baby Jesus, a time for peace on earth and goodwill to all men. But for our children (and ourselves), is Christmas really a time of peace and joy? As a child, the official start of Christmas for me was the arrival of the Sears Wish Book. As an adult, I know Christmas is on its way when stress levels rise, activity increases to frenzied proportions, and I become convinced that my home and family should look like the cover of the Sears catalog!

We are easily caught up in the excitement of the season: the entertaining and partying, the cooking and baking, the shopping and wrapping. We are physically and emotionally— and usually financially—stretched to our limits. Sometimes we hold unrealistic expectations for ourselves and our family that only add to the stress. A four-year-old may easily wonder why such a special holiday leaves no time to read a book or go for a leisurely walk together.

At this busy time of year, concentrate on what is important. Relax and make time for your children and their simple pleasures. Go build a snowman, or read a story by the fire. Bake cookies together, or turn out the lights and watch the Christmas tree. Bundle up for a tour of your neighborhood's Christmas lights, then come home to a mug of steaming cocoa. You probably won't look like the cover of the Sears catalog, but together you will create traditions and make memories that will last a lifetime.

Activity Advent Calendar

Calendar or weekly planner

In the Christian tradition, Advent begins four Sundays before Christmas, but for this idea, the beginning of December is also appropriate. Take out your weekly planner or your wall calendar and mark down a special activity to do with your child each day. For example: stamp and mail your holiday greetings, make some gift wrap together, bake and decorate Christmas cookies, or read a Christmas story by the fire. You can work a lot of your "to do" list into these activities, and planning something special for each day gives you one more way to count down the days to Christmas.

Candy Advent Calendar

This activity continues to be a highlight in our family, and tends to mark the official start of our Advent celebrations. Stock up on your candy and supplies, and invite friends or family to make calendars with you.

Red or green poster board (or construction paper glued to a
  file folder or piece of cardboard)
Pen or marker
Old Christmas cards, rubber stamps, or Christmas stickers
Scissors (optional)
Glue (optional)
25 pieces of wrapped Christmas candy
Ornamental Frosting (see page 365)
Ribbon

Draw a December calendar on the bottom half of a piece of red or green poster board. Have your child cut designs from old Christmas cards and glue them to the top half of the poster board, or decorate it with rubber stamps or Christmas stickers. Use Ornamental Frosting to stick a small piece of wrapped candy onto each grid of the calendar from December 1 through December 25. Lay the calendar flat until the icing sets, then punch a hole in the top and make a hanging loop with a piece of ribbon. Each day your child will have a visual and tasty reminder of the number of days until Christmas.

Christmas Dough Ornaments

Make a batch of dough ornaments (see Baker's Clay or No-Bake Cookie Clay recipes in Appendix A). Glue magnets to the backs for Christmas refrigerator decorations, hang from your Christmas tree as ornaments, give as Christmas gifts, or use as a finishing touch on wrapped gifts.

Paper Snowflakes

White tissue paper cut into squares
Scissors

Fold a square piece of white tissue paper into quarters, then fold into a triangle shape. Cut small shapes along the folded edges, then unfold it to see a snowflake. Tape the snowflake to your window, or around the house for some holiday decorating.

Graham Wafer House

This "gingerbread" house is made with graham wafers and is easier for little hands than one made with traditional gingerbread.

Graham wafers
Cardboard milk carton
Ornamental Frosting (see page 365)
Gumdrops, candy, raisins, chocolate chips, LifeSavers, cereal,
  and other edible decorations

Make Ornamental Frosting to hold the house together. Use the frosting to cement graham wafers to the sides of a cardboard milk carton (remember to cover the frosting with a damp cloth when you're not using it). Allow the frosting to set partially before adding the roof. Decorate with gumdrops, candies, raisins, chocolate chips, LifeSavers, cereal, and so on.

Christmas Place Mats

Used greeting cards
Construction paper or light cardboard
Glue or paste
Clear contact paper

Cut up old greetings cards, glue artwork onto a piece of construction paper or light cardboard, and cover it with clear contact paper for a great Christmas place mat. As a variation, make a Christmas Wish-List Place Mat: Have your child cut out his gift wishes from an old Christmas catalog or magazine and glue them onto a piece of construction paper. Cover the design with clear contact paper and use it as a place mat.

Homemade Gift Wrap

This is a good activity for Christmas or any time of the year. Not only is it environmentally sound, but homemade gift wrap is far more economical and personal than commercially bought wrap, and your child will love to make it, too.

Brown paper bags, butcher paper, or large sheets of paper
Rubber stamps
Ink pads

Cut open brown paper bags, or use butcher paper or large sheets of other paper. Using rubber stamps and ink pads in a variety of colors, your child can decorate the paper according to his personal taste. The colors and rubber stamps can be varied according to the season or occasion.

Christmas Countdown

25 small candy canes, individual pieces of candy, or candy
kisses (for each child)
1 bowl, candy dish, or empty coffee can (for each child)

Place twenty-five small candy canes, kisses, or other special
candy treats into a bowl, candy dish, or empty coffee can.
Beginning December 1, let your child have one treat from his
bowl every day. When he begins to ask "How many days 'til
Christmas?" (and he will!) he can see for himself by counting
the number of candies left in the bowl.

Glitter Balls

Styrofoam balls in various sizes
Glue
Glitter
Small shallow dish
Thread

Pour glitter into a shallow dish. Spread glue evenly over a
Styrofoam ball, then roll it in glitter. Allow the ball to dry,
then attach a thread for hanging on the Christmas tree.

Photo Ornaments

Photograph of your child
Construction paper or cardboard
Scissors
Tape
Glue
Hole punch
Yarn

Draw a star on construction paper, or cut one out of cardboard
and let your child trace it onto the paper. Cut it out. You will
need two stars for each ornament. Cut an opening in the
middle of one paper star and place your child's photo behind
it. Trim the photo to fit, and tape it to the back of the star. Dab
glue onto the back of the star, and press the second paper star
onto it. Punch a hole at the top and thread yarn through; tie it
to form a hanger for your ornament. Write your child's name
and age on the back; he will be proud to hang it on the tree,
year after year.

Dip and Dye Snowflakes

Cone or square-shaped coffee filters (or paper towels cut in
  circles or squares)
Scissors
Small bowls of dye (diluted food coloring or strong tempera
  paint)

Fold coffee filters or paper-towel circles or squares in half,
quarters, thirds, and so on. Dip them into a bowl of dye, blot,
open up, and let dry. When dry, fold again and make snowflakes
by cutting small shapes along the folded edges. Use the snowflakes as a holiday decoration; tape them to your window or
your child's bedroom door.

Christmas Giving

Small toy or gift
Gift-wrap
Tape

Help your child understand the true meaning of Christmas giving. Take him with you to buy a toy or gift for a local charity. Help him wrap it, then deliver it together. On your way home, stop for a muffin or hot chocolate.

Christmas Cloves

Cloves
Orange

Push the pointy ends of the cloves into an orange. Make sure the cloves are firmly attached. The thick ends of the cloves will keep them from being pushed in all the way. Try to keep the cloves' depth as uniform as possible. Cover the entire orange with cloves and enjoy the Christmas scent.

Reindeer Antlers

Brown construction paper
Scissors
Glue

Cut a brown-construction-paper band to fit your child's head. Trace his handprints on the paper, cut them out, and glue them to the headband as reindeer antlers.

319

Holiday Cookies

Rolled cookie dough
Christmas cookie cutters
Colored icing
Sprinkles or other decorative candy

This is one Christmas activity that my sisters and I looked
forward to all year. Make a batch of Cookie Cutouts (page 70),
sugar cookies, or other rolled dough cookies. Use Christmas
cookie cutters to cut out angels, Christmas trees, bells, and so
on. After the cookies have been baked and cooled, set your
child up at the table with bowls of icing in various colors and
all kinds of little goodies for decorating: sprinkles, raisins,
chocolate chips, gumdrops, and so on. He will probably eat
more than he decorates, but this will become a well-cherished
memory.

Christmas Tree Picture

Construction paper in green and other colors
Scissors
Hole punch
Glue
Sequins or glitter

Cut out a Christmas tree from green construction paper. Use a paper hole punch to punch out dots from various colors of construction paper. Glue the dots to your tree for decorations; add sequins or glitter and a star at the top.

Snow Globe

Small baby food jar with lid
Glue gun
Small toys or ornaments that fit into the jar
Water
Gold or silver glitter
¼-inch ribbon

Using a hot glue gun, glue ornaments or small toys to the inside of a baby food jar lid; allow to dry. Have your child fill the jar with water, and add gold or silver glitter. Place the lid on the jar tightly, and glue ribbon to the edge of the lid to seal it. Show your child how to shake up a snowstorm inside the jar.

Thank-You Cards

Construction or other paper
Markers or crayons
Stickers (optional)
Cookie cutters (optional)
Old Christmas cards (optional)
Scissors (optional)
Glue (optional)

Make thank-you cards in advance to help ensure they are sent out promptly when gifts are received. Fold a sheet of paper in half or quarters, and have your child decorate it with crayons or markers, or try some of these ideas:

- Decorate the card with Christmas stickers.
- Trace Christmas cookie cutter shapes.
- Trace around your child's hand.
- Cut up and glue on old Christmas cards.
- Rub a crayon sideways over a card with a raised design (see Christmas Rubbings, page 324).

Christmas Chain

Construction paper in red and green
Glue or paste

Cut strips of red and green construction paper, three to four inches long and one-half to one inch wide. Have your child form a circle with one strip, gluing the ends together. Take the next strip and loop it through the first circle, again gluing the ends together. Tell him to continue looping and gluing until the chain is the length he wants. Use the chain to decorate the Christmas tree, doorway, wall, and so on.

Christmas Rubbings

Christmas card with a raised picture
White paper
Crayons

Lay a piece of white paper over a Christmas card with a raised design on it. Your child can rub a crayon sideways over the paper and watch the design appear.

Rice Krispie Snowman or Christmas Tree

3-quart saucepan
¼ cup margarine or butter
4 cups miniature marshmallows or 40 regular marshmallows
5 cups Rice Krispies
10 to 12 regular marshmallows
Toothpicks
Green food coloring (for tree)
Red cinnamon candies (for tree)
Shredded coconut (for snowman)
Candy for decoration (for snowman)

Melt margarine or butter in a saucepan, then add four cups of marshmallows and cook over low heat, stirring constantly, until syrupy. Remove from heat. If making Christmas trees, add green food coloring until the mixture is fairly dark green. Add Rice Krispies and stir until well coated.

To make Christmas trees, shape into conical forms with buttered hands. When the cones are cooled, stick a toothpick through a marshmallow and stick into the bottom to serve as the trees' base. Decorate with red candies.

To make snowmen, shape into small, medium, and large balls and roll in coconut "snow." Join the balls with toothpicks and decorate with candies.

Paper Plate Wreath

Green paper plate
Red and green tissue paper
Ribbon bow
Scissors
Glue

Cut a hole in the center of a green paper plate. Cut or tear red and green tissue paper into small pieces. Have your child twist the paper or crumple it into small balls and glue them onto the plate. Add a ribbon bow in a contrasting color.

Christmas Card Puzzles

Old Christmas cards
Heavy paper or cardboard
Glue
Scissors

Glue Christmas cards onto heavy paper or cardboard. When dry, cut into puzzles. The puzzle can be very simple and consist of only one card, or it can be more complicated, with two or more cards overlapping to make patterns and designs.

Paper Plate Snowman

Cardboard or three small paper plates
Felt scraps
Glue
Cotton balls (optional)
Paint or markers
Stapler
Scissors

Cut three circles of increasing size from small paper plates or cardboard. Staple the circles together; one plate is the snowman's head and two make his body. Glue on cotton balls if you like. Cut out a scarf, buttons, features, and hat from felt scraps and glue them on the snowman. If you don't use cotton balls, paint the face with paint or markers, then glue on the accessories.

Christmas Bells

Egg carton
Scissors
Yarn, string, or ribbon
Jingle bells
Glue (optional)
Glitter (optional)
Paint (optional)
Aluminum foil (optional)

Cut an egg carton into individual sections; paint, decorate
with glitter, or cover with a small square of aluminum foil.
Make a small hole in the top of each egg cup. Cut yarn, string,
or ribbon into six-inch lengths, and poke one end through the
hole in the top of each egg cup. Thread the bottom piece of
string through a jingle bell and back up through the hole at
the top of the cup. Knot the ends. Hang on doorknobs (you
may need a longer length of string) or on the tree as Christmas
tree ornaments.

Christmas Card Holder

Large green poster board
Small yellow poster board
Scissors
Large colored clothespins or plastic paper clips
Glue
Hole punch
Ribbon
Heavy tape (optional)

Cut a green triangle and a yellow star out of poster board. Glue the star to the top of the green triangle. Glue paper clips or clothespins onto the green triangle Christmas tree. When dry, punch a hole through the poster board where the tree and star meet. Loop a ribbon through the hole and tie a knot. Hang on a hook on the wall, or use heavy tape to attach it to the refrigerator or your child's bedroom door. Attach the Christmas cards you receive to the paper clips or clothespins. (Try adapting this idea for other occasions: Make a Valentine holder by gluing clips onto a big heart cut from red poster board, or glue clips onto a large number "4" to hold cards from your child's fourth birthday.)

Lollipop Tree

Bag of lollipops
Styrofoam cone
Scissors

Divide a bag of lollipops into three groups; one group will be used for the bottom of the tree, one for the middle, and one for the top. Set aside the group for the bottom; cut the sticks of the remaining groups medium length for the middle of the tree, and short for the top of the tree. Show your child how to poke the lollipops into a small Styrofoam cone to make a lollipop tree.

Snowflake Window Decorating

Square of plain or construction paper
Scissors
Tape
Can of spray-on artificial snow

Fold a square piece of paper into quarters, then fold it into a triangle. Cut small shapes along the folded edges, unfold, and tape the snowflake stencil to a window. Spray over the snowflake with artificial snow, then remove it to see the design on the window.

HANUKKAH

Hanukkah, the most joyous and festive of all Jewish holidays, lasts eight days and takes place in December, sometimes early and sometimes late in the month.

Hanukkah, which means "dedication," was first celebrated more than 2,000 years ago. At that time, the Jewish people had just regained control of Judea, their homeland, after many years of repression by cruel foreign kings. Their beloved Temple of Jerusalem, the most important building in Jerusalem and a symbol of God's presence, was not fit for worship. The Jewish people worked hard to restore the Temple and make it pure and sacred once more. Finally it was ready for rededication, but only enough holy oil was found for the Temple menorah to burn for one day. The menorah was lit, the priests rededicated the Temple to God, and the people rejoiced. But their rejoicing was greater still when the oil lasted for eight days instead of one! This is why Hanukkah is also called the Festival of Lights, and why the main focus of the celebration is the lighting of candles every day for eight days on the menorah, a special nine-branch candleholder.

Every year Jews all over the world celebrate Hanukkah. Families gather to light the Hanukkah menorah, remember their ancestors' historic struggle for religious freedom, and recite blessings of thanks to God. Family members exchange gifts, eat special foods, play games, and retell the story of Hanukkah.

Menorah

A menorah consists of nine candles, one for each day of Hanukkah, and one, called the shammash, used to light the other candles.

9 empty thread spools
Playdough
Large birthday candles
Aluminum foil (optional)

Make a Hanukkah menorah using nine empty thread spools to hold the candles. If the candles are a little loose, use some playdough to make them fit snugly. If you want to make the menorah more festive, cover the spools with aluminum foil.

Since a menorah can be any shape or size, use your imagination. Your preschooler can insert candles into playdough or modeling clay that he has shaped into a pleasing design. Try standing candles in a shoe box lid filled with sand, or drill holes for the candles in a tree branch or an interesting piece of driftwood.

Note: Traditionally, you should light your menorah every day and use new candles each time. You will need forty-four candles in total for each menorah you light. Special packages of Hanukkah candles are available during this time of year.

Hanukkah Cookies

Ingredients
Rolled cookie dough

Materials
Paper and pencil
Scissors
Plastic knife

1. Make a batch of dough for Cookie Cutouts (page 70), sugar cookies, gingerbread, or other rolled cookies. Chill.
2. While the dough chills, draw some traditional Hanukkah shapes on paper and cut them out. Some shapes you can try are a Star of David (six-pointed star), a candle, a hammer (the Jews who recaptured their homeland were called Maccabees or "hammerers"), or an elephant (used by the Syrians in their battle with the Jews).
3. Place the paper shapes on the rolled dough and cut around them with a knife. (Your preschooler will be able to use a plastic knife to cut around simple shapes.)

Dreidel

Shin Hay Gimel Noon
שׁ ה ג נ

Dreidel is the name of both the small spinning top used to play this game and of the game itself. Follow these directions to make your own dreidel, then read on for some fun dreidel games.

Small, square milk or juice carton
Plain paper
Tape
Piece of ¼-inch dowel or unsharpened pencil
Pen or marker

Flatten the top of a milk or juice carton and tape it securely. Cover the box with plain paper. On each side, write one of the Hebrew characters shown above, or simply write the letters N, G, H, and S. Push the dowel or pencil through from top to bottom and spin. (The Hebrew characters are the letters shin, hay, gimmel, and noon. These are the first letters in the four words of the Hebrew message *nes gadol hayah sham,* read right to left, which means "A great miracle happened there.")

Dreidel Games

Homemade or store-bought dreidel
Pennies, dried beans, raisins, or other tokens for each player

1. Each player puts one item from his pile of tokens into the center, making a pile called the pot. The first player spins the dreidel; the letter that comes up determines what to do:

   נ (noon) or N—the player does nothing

   ג (gimmel) or G—the player takes the pot and everyone puts in one more item before the next player spins

   ה (hay) or H—the player takes half of the pot

   ש (shin) or S—the player puts one item into the pot.

When the pot is empty or only one token remains, every player puts one item in before the next player spins. The game is over when one player has won everything and everyone else has nothing.

2. Letters of the Hebrew alphabet also have number values, and older children may enjoy keeping score. Noon equals 50, gimmel is 3, heh is 5, and shin is 300. Each player in turn spins the dreidel and wins the number of points corresponding to the Hebrew letter that lands upright.

Potato Latkes

Since oil was an important part of the Temple rededication, eating foods cooked in oil has come to symbolize the victory of the Jews over their enemies. This recipe will make about fifteen *latkes* (Yiddish for "pancake").

Ingredients
5 medium potatoes
1 small onion
2 eggs, beaten
2 tablespoons flour
½ teaspoon salt
¼ teaspoon pepper
Salad oil

Materials
Grater
Medium bowl
Sieve (to drain potatos)
Large frying pan
Slotted spatula
Tablespoon

1. Grate the potatoes and onion and press out the extra liquid.
2. Add the beaten eggs to the potato/onion mixture.
3. Add the flour, salt, and pepper; mix well.
4. Pour about ¼-inch salad oil into the bottom of a large frying pan. Heat the oil, and keep it hot at medium to medium-high heat. Be careful—the oil will splatter.
5. Put batter by the tablespoon into the oil and press each with a slotted spatula to make a thin pancake.
6. When the edges get brown, turn the latke over and cook the other side until golden brown and crisp.
7. Serve warm with sour cream and applesauce.

Star of David Necklace

Yellow, blue, and white construction paper
Pencil or marker
Ruler
Glue
Scissors

Draw two triangles (with two- to three-inch sides) on the yellow construction paper and have your child cut them out. Show him how to make a Star of David by turning one triangle upside down, placing it on top of the other, and gluing them together. Show your child how to make a chain with strips of white and blue construction paper (see Christmas Chain, page 324). Glue the star to the chain to make a necklace or decoration.

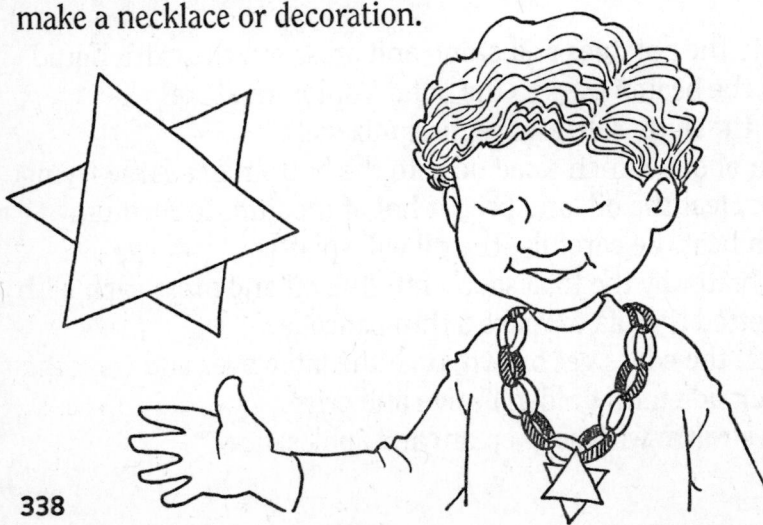

KWANZAA

Kwanzaa is a seven-day holiday celebrated since 1966 by African Americans. Kwanzaa, which takes place each year from December 26th to January 1st, is based on the traditional African winter harvest festival and is not a religious holiday. During this celebration, African Americans reflect upon the ending year and take pride in their African heritage.

Kwanzaa begins the day after Christmas, but the two celebrations are very different. Kwanzaa, which means "first fruit," celebrates the harvest and a way of life handed down by ancestors and parents. Although special handmade gifts or educational games and books are exchanged, families emphasize values rather than gifts. Kwanzaa celebrates seven principles, or values, one for each day of the Kwanzaa week. The principles are *umoja* (unity), *kujichagulia* (self-determination), *ujima* (collective work and responsibility), *ujamaa* (cooperative economics), *nia* (purpose), *kuumba* (creativity), and *imani* (faith). Children are a very important part of the celebration. They light the Kinara (a special, seven-place candle holder), recite and talk about the principles, help prepare the special foods, and present music and dance shows.

On the last day of the holiday, family and friends are invited to attend the Kwanzaa Karamu (kah-RAH-moo). Karamu means feast, and every guest brings food to share as a reminder of the way their African ancestors gathered together to share the fruits of their harvest. The feast traditionally includes greens—such as mustard, kale, and collards—black-eyed peas and rice, peanut dishes, okra, sweet potatoes, and cornbread.

In this section you will find a few simple recipes for foods that might be included in a Kwanzaa Karamu. Try serving the food African style, with pillows or cushions arranged around low tables.

Woven Mat

The woven mat, or mkeka (em-KAY-kah), is the mat on which the other Kwanzaa symbols rest. The mkeka is a symbol of tradition and history.

Black, red, and green construction paper
Scissors
Glue or stapler

Fold black construction paper in half to make a frame for the mat. Show your child how to cut from the folded edge to within one inch of the opposite side. Make an even number of cuts about one inch apart across the entire width of the paper; unfold. Cut one-inch strips of red and green construction paper the length of the frame's width or slightly longer. Show your child how to weave the red and green strips over and under the cuts in the frame. Use glue or a stapler to secure the strips in place along the edge of the frame; trim if necessary.

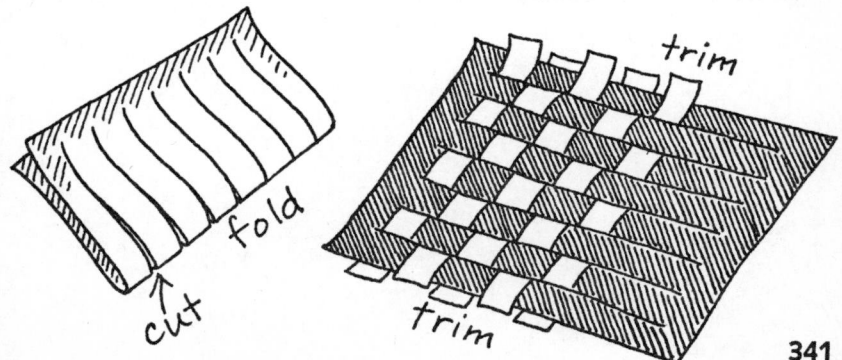

Kwanzaa Flag

The significant colors of Kwanzaa are black, red, and green:
Black symbolizes the color of the people, red their continuing
struggle, and green their hope for the future.

Paper
Red, green, and black crayons or markers

Divide a piece of drawing paper horizontally into three equal
parts (either by drawing lines or by folding the paper into
three equal sections). Have your child color the top section
red, the middle section black, and the bottom section green to
create his own Kwanzaa flag.

African Beads

Zawadi (zah-WAH-dee) are the gifts given as rewards for having lived according to the Kwanzaa values during the year. Here is a simple way to make a necklace or bracelet that can be given as a zawadi gift.

Ziti noodles
Black, red, and green tempera paint (optional)
Paintbrushes
Glitter, large buttons, plastic beads (optional)
Shoelace, ribbon, or thin cord
Pine cone (optional)

Paint ziti noodles with tempera paint and sprinkle with glitter while the paint is still wet (or dye them using the Pasta Dye recipe, page 364). When the paint is dry, thread the shoelace, ribbon, or cord through the noodles, buttons, and beads to create a unique necklace or bracelet. You can also start with a pine cone or other interesting object tied onto the middle of the shoelace, ribbon, or cord, then thread the noodles, beads, or buttons on either side of the centerpiece in an attractive design.

African Animal Necklace

This necklace can be given as a zawadi gift, or your child can make it for himself.

No-Bake Craft Clay (see page 360)
Animal cookie cutters (optional)
String or thread
Black satin cord

Have your child shape clay into African animals, such as elephants, lions, zebras, and giraffes. If you like, use animal cookie cutters to make the shapes. You can divide the clay into batches, and add food coloring for each animal. Make a hole at the top of each animal shape for the thread. Once the clay is dry, attach each animal to a black satin cord with string or thread, making a knot to keep each animal in place.

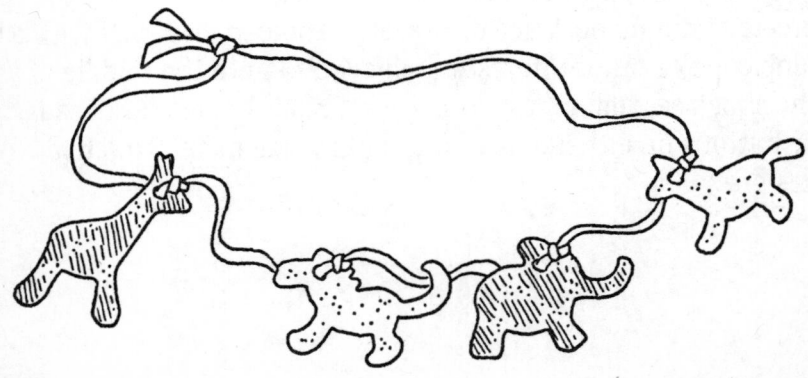

North African Orange Salad

Ingredients
2 cups lettuce, shredded
1 large onion, peeled and thinly sliced
8 Greek olives, pitted and sliced
2 large oranges, peeled and thinly sliced
2 tablespoons olive oil
2 tablespoons lemon juice
⅛ teaspoon salt
⅛ teaspoon pepper

Materials
Salad bowl and mixing utensils
Small bowl

1. Combine the lettuce, onion, and olives in a salad bowl; mix until evenly distributed.
2. Arrange orange slices on top.
3. Mix oil, lemon juice, salt, and pepper in a small bowl to make a salad dressing. Pour dressing over salad and refrigerate until serving time. Serves 4.

Liberian Rice Bread

Ingredients
2 cups cream of rice cereal
4 tablespoons sugar
1 teaspoon baking soda
1 teaspoon salt
½ teaspoon nutmeg
3 cups mashed bananas
1 cup water
½ cup vegetable oil
Butter or margerine

Materials
Large mixing bowl
Mixer (optional)
8-by-12-inch or a 9-inch round cake
Spoon

1. Preheat the oven to 400 degrees.
2. In a large mixing bowl, mix together (by hand or with a mixer) the cream of rice cereal, sugar, baking soda, salt, and nutmeg until well blended.
3. Add bananas, water, and vegetable oil. Stir until the mixture is smooth, about 3 minutes.
4. Spoon the batter into a round cake pan. Bake for 30 minutes or until lightly browned. Serve hot with butter or margerine.

Caribbean Fruit Punch

Ingredients
2½ cups lemonade
1 cup orange juice
1 cup pineapple juice
1 cup papaya juice
1 cup guava juice

Materials
Large pitcher or punch bowl
Long spoon for mixing

1. Mix all the juices together in a large pitcher or punch bowl.
2. Serve over ice.

Senegalese Cookies

Called *cinq centimes* (five-cent cookies) in the marketplaces of Dakar, these cookies are simple to make and tasty to eat.

1 16-ounce package sugar cookies (or make your own)
1 cup smooth peanut butter
1 cup chopped peanuts

1. Spread each sugar cookie with peanut butter.
2. Sprinkle with chopped peanuts.

Appendix A

Basic Craft Recipes

"There is so much to teach, and the time goes so fast."
—*Erma Bombeck*

Even at a very young age, your child can begin to develop her own creative skills and understand the artistic work of others. Visual art is not limited to paper and paint, but includes many different media. The craft materials in this section are essential for every child's artwork: paint, glue, paste, modeling compounds, and more.

PAINT

Each of the following recipes will produce a good paint for your child to use. Each varies in the ingredients required and the method used, so choose one that best suits the supplies you have on hand and the time you have available.

When mixing paint, keep in mind the age of the artist; as a general rule, the younger the artist, the thicker the paint (and brushes) should be. Paint should be stored covered; small plastic spill-proof paint containers are available at your local art supply store. These come with an airtight lid for storage, hold brushes upright nicely without tipping, and, at several dollars each, are well worth the purchase price.

Flour-Based Poster Paint
¼ cup flour
Saucepan
1 cup water
Small jars or plastic containers
3 tablespoons powdered tempera paint
2 tablespoons water
½ teaspoon liquid starch or liquid detergent (optional)

Measure flour into a saucepan. Slowly add 1 cup water to make the paste smooth. Heat, stirring constantly, until mixture begins to thicken. Cool. Measure a quarter cup of the flour paste into a small jar or plastic container. Add three tablespoons powdered tempera paint and two tablespoons water for each color. For an opaque finish, add liquid starch. For a glossy finish, add liquid detergent. Store covered.

Detergent Poster Paint
1 tablespoon clear liquid detergent
2 teaspoons powdered tempera paint
Small jars or plastic containers

For each color, mix together liquid detergent and powdered tempera paint in a amall jar or plastic container. This makes enough for one painting session.

Condensed Milk Paint

Bowl or other container
1 cup condensed milk
Food coloring

In a bowl, mix one cup of condensed milk with drops of food coloring to make a very glossy, brightly colored paint. This paint is not intended to be eaten, but it won't harm any child who decides to make a snack of it.

Homemade Face Paint

This face paint is suitable for painting designs with a small brush.

Bowl or other container
1 teaspoon corn starch
½ teaspoon cold cream
½ teaspoon water
Food coloring
Small paintbrush

In a bowl, stir together corn starch and cold cream until well blended. Add water and stir. Add food coloring, one drop at a time until you get the desired color. Paint designs on face with a small paintbrush; remove with soap and water. Store paint in a covered plastic container or a baby food jar.

Halloween Face Paint

Bowl or other container
1 tablespoon solid shortening
2 tablespoons cornstarch
Food coloring
Sponge (optional)
Small paintbrush (optional)

In a bowl, mix shortening and cornstarch together until smooth. Add food coloring, one drop at a time, until you get the desired color. Use a sponge or your fingers to apply paint over a large area, such as an entire face. To paint a design with a small brush, thin the paint with a little water first. Remove with soap and water. Store paint in a baby food jar or a covered plastic container.

Egg Yolk Paint

This recipe is suitable for painting edible cookies.

1 egg yolk
¼ teaspoon water
Food coloring
Bowl or other container
Paintbrush

In a bowl, mix one egg yolk with a quarter teaspoon water and lots of food coloring. Use a paintbrush to paint freshly baked cookies; return cookies to oven until egg solidifies.

FINGERPAINT

Each of the following recipes produces a good fingerpaint, however the ingredients and mixing methods vary. Choose one that is suitable for the ingredients you have on hand and the time you have available.

Cornstarch Fingerpaint
3 tablespoons sugar
½ cup cornstarch
Medium saucepan
2 cups cold water
Muffin tin or small cups
Spoon
Food coloring
Soap flakes or liquid dishwashing detergent

Mix sugar and cornstarch in a medium saucepan over low heat. Add cold water and continue stirring until the mixture is thick. Remove from heat. Divide the mixture into four or five portions, spooning them into sections of a muffin tin or small cups. Add a drop or two of food coloring and a pinch of soap flakes or a drop of liquid dishwashing detergent to each portion. Use a different color for each cup. Stir and let cool. Store covered in an airtight container.

Flour Fingerpaint
1 cup flour
2 tablespoons salt
1½ cups cold water
1¼ cups hot water
Saucepan
Whisk or rotary beater
Food coloring or powdered tempera paint

Put flour and salt in a saucepan. Add cold water and beat with a whisk or rotary beater until smooth. Add hot water and boil until mixture is thick. Beat again until smooth. Keep in the refrigerator and color as needed with food coloring or powdered tempera paint.

PLAYDOUGH

Everyone seems to have their own favorite playdough recipe, and many old favorites have been included here. Some require cooking, some are no-cook, some are meant to be eaten, and some are not. Choose the recipe that best suits your requirements and the ingredients you have on hand. Store playdough in a covered container or plastic bag. If it sweats a little, just add more flour.

Oatmeal Playdough

This is an ideal playdough for your child to make herself. It must be refrigerated, and it doesn't last as long as cooked playdough.

1 part flour
1 part water
2 parts oatmeal
Bowl

Combine all ingredients in a bowl; mix well and knead until smooth. This is not intended to be edible, but it will not hurt kids if they eat it.

Uncooked Playdough

1 cup cold water
1 cup salt
2 teaspoons vegetable oil
Tempera paint or food coloring
3 cups flour
2 tablespoons cornstarch
Bowl

Mix water, salt, oil, and enough tempera paint to make a bright color. Gradually add flour and cornstarch until the mixture reaches the consistency of bread dough.

Colored Playdough
1 cup water
1 tablespoon vegetable oil
½ cup salt
1 tablespoon cream of tartar
Food coloring
Saucepan
1 cup flour

Combine water, oil, salt, cream of tartar, and food coloring in a saucepan and heat until warm. Remove from heat and add flour. Stir, then knead until smooth. Keep in mind that the cream of tartar makes this dough long-lasting—up to six months or longer—so resist the temptation to leave it out if you don't have it on hand. This dough should be stored in an airtight container or a Ziploc bag. Do not refrigerate.

Salt Playdough
1 cup salt
1 cup water
½ cup flour
Saucepan

Combine salt, water, and flour in a saucepan; mix and cook over medium heat. Remove from heat when mixture is thick and rubbery. As the mixture cools, knead in enough flour to make the dough workable.

Peanut Butter Playdough
Definitely an edible playdough!

18 ounces peanut butter
6 tablespoons honey
Nonfat dry milk or milk plus flour
Cocoa or carob for chocolate flavor (optional)
Bowl
Edible treats for decoration

Combine all ingredients in a bowl and mix, adding enough dry milk or milk plus flour to reach the consistency of bread dough. Add cocoa or carob, if desired. Shape, decorate with other edible treats, and eat!

Kool-Aid Playdough
½ cup salt
2 cups water
Saucepan
Food coloring, tempera powder, or Kool-Aid for color
2 tablespoons salad oil
2 cups sifted flour
2 tablespoons alum (available at your grocery or drugstore)

Boil salt in water in a saucepan until the salt dissolves. Remove from heat and tint with food coloring, tempera powder, or Kool-Aid. Add salad oil, flour, and alum. Knead or process until smooth. This dough will last two months or longer.

CLAY

Use the following recipes to produce clay that can be rolled or shaped into ornaments. The drying methods vary, either overnight or in the oven. When hard, ornaments can be painted and preserved with acrylic.

Baker's Clay
4 cups flour
1 cup salt
1 teaspoon powdered alum
1½ cups water
Food coloring (optional)
Large bowl
Cookie sheet
Cookie cutters (optional)
Plastic straw (optional)
Fine wire (optional)
Fine sandpaper
Plastic-based poster paint, acrylic paint, or markers
Clear shellac, acrylic spray, or clear nail polish

Mix all ingredients in a large bowl. If the dough is too dry, work in another tablespoon of water with your hands. Dough can be colored by dividing it into several parts and kneading a drop or two of food coloring into each part. Roll or mold as desired.

To roll: Roll dough one-eighth-inch thick on a lightly floured surface. Cut with cookie cutters dipped in flour. Make a hole in the top, quarter-inch down, for hanging, by using the end of a plastic straw dipped in flour. Shake the dots of clay from the straw and press onto the dough shape as decorations.

To mold: Shape dough no more than half-inch thick into figures, such as flowers, fruits, animals, and so on. Insert a fine wire in each for hanging.

Bake ornaments on an ungreased cookie sheet for about thirty minutes in a 250 degree oven. Turn and bake another one and a half hours until hard and dry. Remove and cool, then sand lightly with fine sandpaper until smooth. Paint both sides with plastic-based poster paint, acrylic paint, or markers. Allow paint to dry and seal with clear shellac, acrylic spray, or clear nail polish.

Makes about five dozen two-and-a-half-inch ornaments.

Modeling Clay
2 cups salt
⅔ cups water
Saucepan
1 cup cornstarch
½ cup cold water

Stir salt and water in a saucepan over heat four to five minutes. Remove from heat; add cornstarch and cold water. Stir until smooth; return to heat and cook until thick. Store in a plastic bag.

No-Bake Cookie Clay
These ornaments are not edible!

2 cups salt
⅔ cup water
Medium saucepan
1 cup cornstarch
½ cup cold water
Rolling pin
Cookie cutters
Straw
Paint, glitter, and other decorative materials

Mix salt with ⅔ cup water in a medium saucepan. Stir and boil. Add cornstarch and ½ cup cold water and stir. If the mixture doesn't get thick, set it back on the stove. Sprinkle some extra cornstarch onto the table, roll out the dough with a rolling pin, and cut with cookie cutters. Use a straw to make a hole at the top for hanging. Dry and decorate with paint, glitter, and so on.

No-Bake Craft Clay
1 cup cornstarch
1¼ cups cold water
2 cups baking soda (1 pound)
Saucepan
Food coloring (optional)
Plate

Damp cloth
Tempera paints or acrylic paints (optional)
Shellac, clear acrylic, or clear nail polish

Combine cornstarch, cold water, and baking soda in a saucepan; stir over medium heat for about four minutes until the mixture thickens to a moist mashed-potato consistency. For color, add a few drops of food coloring to the water before it is mixed with the starch and soda. Remove from heat, turn out onto a plate and cover with a damp cloth until cool. Knead as you would dough. Shape as desired or store in an airtight container or plastic bag. Objects may be left to dry then painted with tempera paints or acrylics. Dip in shellac, spray with clear acrylic, or brush with clear nail polish to seal.

Bread Clay
6 slices white bread
6 tablespoons white glue
½ teaspoon detergent or 2 teaspoons glycerin
Food coloring
Paintbrush
Acrylic paints, acrylic spray, or clear nail polish

Remove the crusts from white bread and knead the bread with glue plus either detergent or glycerin until the mixture is no longer sticky. Separate into portions and tint with food coloring. Let your child shape the clay. Brush the finished product with equal parts glue and water for a smooth appearance. Let dry overnight to harden. Use acrylic paints, acrylic spray, or clear nail polish to seal and preserve.

GLUE and PASTE

The following glue and paste recipes use a variety of ingredients and methods. Choose the one that best suits your project. For variety, add food coloring to glue before using. Store all products in airtight containers in the refrigerator.

Glue

¾ cup water
2 tablespoons corn syrup
1 teaspoon white vinegar
Small saucepan
Small bowl
2 tablespoons cornstarch
¾ cup cold water

Mix water, corn syrup, and white vinegar in a small saucepan. Bring to a full, rolling boil. In a small bowl, mix cornstarch with cold water. Add this mixture slowly to the hot mixture, stirring constantly until the mixture returns to a boil. Boil for one minute, then remove from heat. When slightly cooled, pour into another container and let stand overnight before using.

Homemade Paste
½ cup flour
Cold water
Saucepan
Flavoring and/or food coloring (optional)

Add some cold water to the flour until it is as thick as cream. Simmer and stir in a saucepan for five minutes. Add a few drops of flavoring and/or food coloring, if desired. This recipe makes a wet, messy paste that takes a while to dry.

Papier-Mâché Paste
1 cup water
¼ cup flour
5 cups lightly boiling water
Large saucepan

Mix flour into one cup of water until the mixture is thin and runny. Stir this mixture into the lightly boiling water. Gently boil and stir for two to three minutes. Cool before using.

No-Cook Paste
½ cup flour
Water
Salt
Bowl

Mix flour with water until gooey. Add a pinch of salt; stir.

OTHER CRAFT RECIPES

Use the following recipes to make interesting materials for use in various arts and crafts projects.

Colorful Creative Salt
½ cup salt
5 to 6 drops food coloring
Wax paper or microwave-safe container and microwave

Add food coloring to salt and stir well. Cook in a microwave for one to two minutes, or spread on wax paper and let air dry. Store in an airtight container. Use as you would glitter.

Pasta Dye
½ cup rubbing alcohol
Food coloring
Bowl
Variety of dry pasta
Newspapers
Wax paper
Spoon

Mix alcohol and food coloring in a bowl. Add small amounts of various dry pasta to the liquid and gently mix. The larger the pasta, the longer it will take to absorb the color. Dry on newspapers covered with wax paper.

Egg Dye

¼ teaspoon food coloring
¾ cup hot water
1 tablespoon white vinegar
Bowl or cup
Eggs

Measure all liquids into a bowl or a cup and mix. Use different food coloring in each container for desired shades. Soak eggs in the dyes until they reach the desired shades.

Ornamental Frosting

This frosting works like an edible glue; use for gingerbread houses or other food projects that you want to eat!

3 egg whites
1 teaspoon cream of tartar
1 pound powdered sugar, sifted (about 4 cups)
Bowl
Egg beater
Damp cloth

Beat egg whites with cream of tartar in a bowl until stiff peaks form. Add sifted icing sugar and continue beating until mixture is thick and holds its shape. Cover with a damp cloth when not in use. This mixture can be made several hours or the day before using. Store in an airtight container in the refrigerator.

Appendix B

Crazy Can Activities

The following activities are suitable for a Crazy Can (see Chapter 1). These activities are suggested because they require no special materials, need no time-consuming preparation or cleanup, and above all, demand a minimal amount of adult participation. Some of these ideas require a little advance planning (i.e., have a map or clues prepared in advance for the Indoor Treasure Hunt). These activities will provide you with an instant remedy when things start to get crazy, or when there's just "nothing to do." (The number following each activity refers to the page on which that activity is found.)

Appendix C

Gifts for Kids to Make and Give

Most kids love to give gifts almost as much as they love to receive them, and the excitement is usually intensified if the gift is something they have made themselves. The following activities provide fun and easy ways for kids to personalize their gift-giving. The number following each activity refers to the page on which that activity is found.

The following activities can be used to create unique and personal greetings cards and gift wrap

Appendix D

Best Books for Young Children

The following books are suggested for children up to age eight (many are loved by much older children, too), either for reading by or to the child. This list has been compiled from several sources. *Timeless Classics*, published by the National Endowment for the Humanities, is a compilation of tried-and-true titles. These are books published in 1960 or earlier that have been the favorite of at least one previous generation. Another source is *Reading for the Love of It* by Michele Landsberg (1987, Prentice Hall Press/a division of Simon & Schuster, New York; reprinted by permission of the publisher), an excellent guide to the best books for children of all ages. A final source is the bookshelves in my own children's rooms, favorite volumes that have been read over and over and over again.

Aardema, Verna. *The Vingananee and the Tree Toad; Why Mosquitoes Buzz in People's Ears*
Aesop. *Aesop's Fables*
Ahlberg, Janet and Allen. *Each Peach Pear Plum*
Alderson, Sue Ann. *Bonnie McSmithers, You're Driving Me Dithers*
Allen, Jeffrey. *Mary Alice, Operator Number Nine*

Atwater, Richard and Florence. *Mr. Popper's Penguins*
Bemelmans, Ludwig. Madeline series
Brooke, Leslie L. *Johnny Crow's Party*
Brown, Margaret Wise. *Goodnight Moon*
Brunhoff, Jean de. *The Story of Babar*
Burningham, John. *Cannonball Simp; Harquin, the Fox Who Went Down to the Valley; Would You Rather?*
Burton, Virginia Lee. *Mike Mulligan and His Steam Shovel; The Little House*
Caldicott, Randolph. *Hey, Diddle Diddle*
Clifton, Lucille. *Don't You Remember?*
Crowther, Robert. *The Most Amazing Hide-and-Seek Alphabet Book*
Dalgleish, Alice. *The Bears on Hemlock Mountain; The Courage of Sarah Noble*
Eastman, P.D. *Are You My Mother?; Go, Dog, Go*
Flack, Marjorie. *The Story about Ping*
Freeman, Don. *Corduroy*
Gag, Wanda. *Millions of Cats*
Godden, Rumer. *The Mousewife*
Goffstein, M.B. *Our Snowman*
Grahame, Kenneth. *The Reluctant Dragon*
Haywood, Carolyn. Betsy series
Hoban, Russell. *Bread and Jam for Frances*
Hutchins, Pat. *Rosie's Walk*
Jonas, Ann. *The Trek*

Keats, Ezra Jack. *Goggles!*
Kellogg, Steven. *The Island of the Skog*
Kipling, Rudyard. *Just So Stories for Little Children*
Kovalski, Maryann. *Brenda and Edward*
Kraus, Robert. *Herman the Helper; Whose Mouse Are You?*
Leaf, Munro. *The Story of Ferdinand*
Lear, Edward. *The Book of Nonsense*
MacDonald, Betty. *Mrs. Piggle-Wiggle*
Marshall, James. *George and Martha*
McCloskey, Robert. *Blueberries for Sal; Make Way for Ducklings*
McDermott, Gerald. *Papagayo, the Mischief-Maker*
Meyer, Mercer. Little Critter series
Milne, A.A. *The House at Pooh Corner; Now We Are Six; When We Were Very Young; Winnie-the-Pooh*
Minaruk, Else Holmelund. *Little Bear*
Mosel, Arlene. *The Funny Little Woman; Tikkie Tikki Tembo*
Munsch, Robert. *Love You Forever; The Paperbag Princess*
Nicoll, Helen. *Meg and Mog*
Ormerod, Jan. *Moonlight; Sunshine*
Perrault, Charles. *Cinderella*
Pinkwater, Manus. *Three Big Hogs*
Potter, Beatrix. *The Tale of Peter Rabbit*
Rey, H.A. Curious George series
Segal, Lore. *Tell Me a Mitzi; Tell Me a Trudy*
Selden, George. *The Cricket in Times Square*
Sendak, Maurice. *Where the Wild Things Are*

Seuss, Dr. *Green Eggs and Ham; The Cat in the Hat; The 500 Hats of Bartholomew Cubbins*

Shulevitz, Uri. *One Monday Morning*

Stamm, Claus. *Three Strong Women*

Steig, William. *Brave Irene; Sylvester and the Magic Pebble*

Stevenson, James. *Could Be Worse!*

Stevenson, John. *Clams Can't Sing*

Stevenson, Robert Louis. *A Child's Garden of Verses*

Viorst, Judith. *Alexander and the Terrible, Horrible, No Good, Very Bad Day*

Waber, Bernard. Lyle the Crocodile series

Wagner, Jenny. *The Bunyip of Berkeley's Creek*

Wallace, Ian. *Chin Chiang and the Dragon's Dance*

Watson, Clyde. *Applebet, an ABC*

Wells, Rosemary. *Noisy Nora*

Wildsmith, Brian. *Cat on the Mat*

Williams, Jay. *Everyone Knows What a Dragon Looks Like*

Williams, Margery. *The Velveteen Rabbit*

Williams, Vera B. *Cherries and Cherry Pits*

Wood, Audrey. *Sid and Sol; The Napping House*

Wynne-Jones, Tim. *Zoom at Sea*

Yeoman, John. *The Wild Washerwoman*

Yorinks, Arthur. *Hey, Al*

Zemach, Harve. *The Judge*

Zion, Gene. *Harry the Dirty Dog*

Zolotow, Charlotte. *Mister Rabbit and the Lovely Present*

Appendix E

Resources

This book is a combination of personal experience, contributions from friends and family, and ideas and information gathered from the books and government publications listed below.

Baby Games, by Elaine Martin, Stoddart Publishing, 1988.

Becoming a Nation of Readers: What Parents Can Do, by D.C. Heath and Company and the U.S. Department of Education, 1988.

Celebrating Kwanzaa, by Diane Hoyt-Goldsmith, Holiday House, 1993.

Children's Art & Crafts, by Nancy Lewis Bartlett, The Australian Women's Weekly Home Library, Australian Consolidated Press, 1991.

Creative Family Times, by Allen & Connie Hadidian, Will & Lindy Wilson, Moody Press, 1989.

Dance and Your Child, by The National Dance Association and The National Endowment for the Arts, 1991.

Family Math, by Stenmark, Thompson and Cossey, University of California, 1986 (For information contact: Lawrence Hall of Science, University of California Berkeley, CA 94720 Attn: FAMILY MATH).

Feed Me! I'm Yours, by Vicky Lansky, Meadowbrook Press, 1974.

From Words to Stories, Teachers and Writers Collaborative and The National Endowment for the Arts, 1991.

Hanukkah Book, The, by Marilyn Burns, Fourwinds Press, 1981.

Help! I Have a Preschool Child!!!, by Kandi Arnold, Andrea Devin, Dale Sprowl, Garborg's Heart 'N Home, 1990.

Help Your Child Become a Good Reader, by U.S. Department of Education.

Helping Your Child Learn Geography, by U.S. Department of Education, 1990.

Helping Your Child Learn Math, by U.S. Department of Education, 1993.

Helping Your Child Learn to Read, by U.S. Department of Education, 1993.

Honey for a Child's Heart, by Gladys Hunt, Zondervan, 1989

Jewish Holidays, by Susan Gold-Purdy, J.B. Lipincott Company, 1969.

Kwanzaa, by Deborah M. Newton Chocolate, Children's Press, 1990.

Learning about Fall and Winter Holidays, by Jeri A. Carroll and Candace B. Wells, Good Apple Inc., 1988.

Light Another Candle, by Miriam Chaikin, Clarion Books, 1981.

Lollipop Grapes & Clothespin Critters, by Robyn Freedman Spitzman, Addison-Wesley Publishing, 1985.

Mother's Almanac, The, by Marguerite Kelly and Elia Parsons, Doubleday, 1975.

Mother's Manual for Summer Survival, A, by Kathy Peel and Joy Mahaffey, Focus on the Family Publishing, 1989.

Music and Your Child's Education, by The Music Educators National Conference and The National Endowment for the Arts, 1991.

Papier-Mâché Artistry, by Dona Z. Meilach, General Publishing, 1971.

Prime Time Together ... With Kids, by Donna Erickson, Augsburg Fortress, 1989.

Rainy Day Activities for Preschoolers, by Ann Marie Connolly and Helen Gibson, Mercer Island Preschool Association, 1988.

Read-Aloud Handbook, The, by Jim Trelease, Penguin Books, 1995.

Reading for the Love of It, by Michele Landsberg, Prentice Hall Press, 1987.

Seven Days of Kwanzaa, The, by Angela Shelf Medearis, Scholastic Inc., 1994.

Sunset Children's Crafts, Lane Publishing Co., 1976.

Theater and Children, by the American Alliance for Theater and Education and The National Endowment for the Arts, 1991.

Timeless Classics, by the National Endowment for the Humanities, 1991.

What to Do After You Turn Off the TV, by Frances Moore
  Lappé, Random House, 1985.
You Can Help Your Young Child Learn Mathematics, by the
  U.S. Department of Education, 1991.
Your Baby & Child From Birth to Age Five, by Penelope
  Leach, Random House, 1989.
Your Child and the Visual Arts, by The National Art Education
  Association and The National Endowment for the Arts, 1991.

The United States General Services Administration makes
available many free and low-cost federal publications of
consumer interest, including many on learning activities and
parenting. For a free catalog write to: Consumer Information
Center-2C, P.O. Box 100, Pueblo, Colorado 81002.

Index

"When you are dealing with a child, keep all your wits about you, and sit on the floor." —*Austin O'Malley*

The Joy of Parenthood

by Jan Blaustone

This book contains hundreds of warm and inspirational "nuggets" of wisdom to help prepare parents for the pleasures and challenges ahead. Throughout the book, 24 touching black-and-white photos help convey the joy of parenthood and make this a delightful book to give or receive.

Order #3500

Familiarity Breeds Children

Selected by Bruce Lansky

Lansky has created a humor book for parents that will delight and revive them. This collection is a treasury of the most outrageous and clever things ever said about raising children by world-class comedians and humorists, including Roseanne, Erma Bombeck, Bill Cosby, Dave Barry, Mark Twain, Fran Lebowitz, and others. Filled with entertaining photographs, it makes the perfect gift for any parents you know—including yourself. Originally entitled *The Funny Side of Parenthood*.

Order #4015

Moms Say the Funniest Things!
by Bruce Lansky

Lansky has collected moms' most popular lines for dealing with "emergencies" like getting the kids out of bed, cleaned, dressed, to school, to the dinner table, undressed, and back to bed. It includes all-time winners like "Put on clean underwear—you never know when you'll be in an accident" and "If God had wanted you to fool around, He would have written the 'Ten Suggestions.'" A fun gift for mom!

Order #4280

Dads Say the Dumbest Things!
by Bruce Lansky and K. L. Jones

Lansky and Jones have collected all the greatest lines dads have ever used to get kids to stop fighting in the car, feed the pet, turn off the TV while doing homework, and get home from a date before curfew. It includes winners like "What do you want a pet for—you've got a sister" and "When I said 'feed the goldfish,' I didn't mean feed them to the cat." A fun gift for dad!

Order #4220

Grandma Knows Best, But No One Ever Listens!

by Mary McBride

McBride offers much-needed advice for new grandmas
on how to

- show baby photos to anyone at any time;
- get out of babysitting or, if stuck, "housebreak" the kids before they wreck the house;
- advise the daughter-in-law without being banned from her home.

The perfect gift for Grandma. Phyllis Diller says it's "harder to put down than a new grandchild."

Order #4009

Practical Parenting Tips
by Vicki Lansky

Here's the #1-selling collection of helpful hints for parents with babies and small children. It contains 1,001 parent-tested tips for dealing with diaper rash, nighttime crying, toilet training, temper tantrums, and traveling with tots. It will help parents save time, trouble, and money.

Order #1180

Feed Me! I'm Yours
by Vicki Lansky

Now expanded, updated, and revised for the '90s! This best-selling baby and toddler food cookbook has sold millions of copies. It's a must-have book for all new parents. More than 200 child-tested recipes. Comb-bound for easy use.

"A well-written, homorous combination cookbook and advice book that makes the job of parenting a lot easier and enjoyable."
—*Milwaukee Journal*

Order #1109

Gentle Discipline

by Dawn Lighter, M.A.

Dawn Lighter has written a breakthrough book that will change the way parents think about and practice "discipline." Most parents think of discipline as something to do after children misbehave. Lighter's book provides 50 simple, effective ways to teach children good behavior—so they won't misbehave.

Order #1085

Discipline Without Shouting or Spanking

by Jerry Wyckoff, Ph.D. and Barbara C. Unell

Do you know all the theories about child rearing but still have trouble coping with some of your child's misbehavior? You'll love this book! It covers the 30 most common forms of misbehavior from whining to throwing temper tantrums. You'll find clear, practical advice on what to do, what not to do, and how to prevent each problem from recurring.

Order #1079

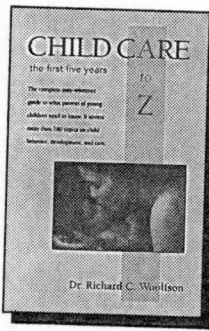

Child Care A to Z
by Dr. Richard C. Woolfson

This easy-to-understand reference contains up-to-date information on 170 topics that every parent needs to know. It is organized alphabetically to help parents find answers to questions about their child's physical, emotional, and intellectual development. Dr. Woolfson is known as the Dr. Spock of the United Kingdom, and his child-care experience is now available to American parents.
Order #1010

How to Read Your Child Like a Book
by Lynn Weiss, Ph.D.

This is the first book that helps parents interpret their child's behavior by teaching parents what their child is thinking. Dr. Lynn Weiss, a nationally recognized expert on child development, explains 50 different behaviors of young children from birth to age 6. You will gain new insight and understanding into such behaviors as boundary testing, selfishness, and temper tantrums.
Order #1145

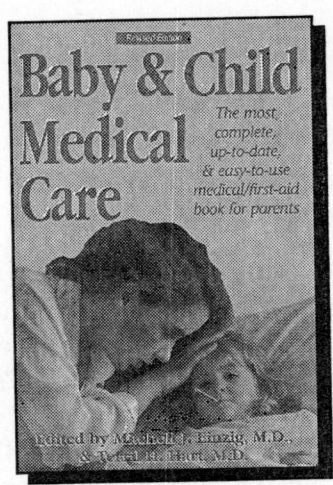

Baby & Child Medical Care

Edited by Mitchell J. Einzig, M.D.,
and Terril H. Hart, M.D.

Every first-aid or medical problem your child suffers from seems like an emergency. Newly revised and updated, this book provides illustrated step-by-step instructions that show you what to do and tell you when to call your doctor. Its visual approach makes this book much easier to use than Dr. Spock's.

Order #1159

The Toddler's Busy Book

by Trish Kuffner.

This book contains 365 activities (one for each day of the year) for one-and-a-half- to three-year-olds using things found around the home. It shows parents and day-care providers how to:

- prevent boredom during even the longest stretches of bad weather with ideas for indoor play, kitchen activities, and arts and crafts projects;

- save money by making your own paints, playdough, craft clays, glue, paste, and other arts and crafts supples;

- stimulate a child's natural curiosity with entertaining math, language, and motor-skills activies.

Order #1250

Notes

Notes

Order Form

Qty.	Title	Author	Order No.	Unit Cost (U.S. $)	Total
	Baby/Child Emergency First Aid	Einzig, M.	1381	$8.00	
	Baby & Child Medical Care	Einzig/Hart	1159	$9.00	
	Child Care A to Z	Woolfson, R.	1010	$11.00	
	Dads Say the Dumbest Things!	Lansky/Janes	4220	$6.00	
	Discipline w/o Shouting/Spanking	Wykoff/Unell	1079	$6.00	
	Familiarity Breeds Children	Lansky, B.	4015	$7.00	
	Feed Me! I'm Yours	Lansky, V.	1109	$9.00	
	Gentle Discipline	Lighter, D.	1085	$6.00	
	Grandma Knows Best	McBride, M.	4009	$7.00	
	How to Read Child Like a Book	Weiss, L.	1145	$8.00	
	Joy of Parenthood	Blaustone, J.	3500	$7.00	
	Moms Say the Funniest Things!	Lansky, B.	4280	$6.00	
	Practical Parenting Tips	Lansky, V.	1180	$8.00	
	Preschooler's Busy Book	Kuffner, T.	6055	$9.95	
	Toddler's Busy Book	Kuffner, T.	1250	$9.95	
	Very Best Baby Name Book	Lansky, B.	1030	$8.00	
				Subtotal	
		Shipping and Handling (see below)			
		MN residents add 6.5% sales tax			
				Total	

YES! Please send me the books indicated above. Add $2.00 shipping and handling for the first book with a retail price up to $9.99 or $3.00 for the first book with a retail price over $9.99. Add $1.00 shipping and handling for each additional book. All orders must be prepaid. Most orders are shipped within two days by U.S. Mail (7–9 delivery days). Rush shipping is available for an extra charge. Overseas postage will be billed. **Quantity discounts available upon request.**

Send book(s) to:

Name _____ Address _____

City _____State _____ Zip _____Telephone (_____)_____

Payment via:
☐ Check or money order payable to Meadowbrook Press (No cash or C.O.D.'s please)
☐ Visa (for orders over $10.00 only)   ☐ MasterCard (for orders over $10.00 only)
Account # _____ Signature _____ Exp. Date _____

A FREE Meadowbrook Press catalog is available upon request.
You can also phone us for orders of $10.00 or more at 1-800-338-2232.

Mail to: Meadowbrook Press, 5451 Smetana Drive, Minnetonka, MN 55343
Phone 952-930-1100   Toll -Free 800-338-2232   Fax 952-930-1940
For more information (and fun) visit our website: www.meadowbrookpress.com